BEFORE AND BEYOND
THE NIAGARA MOVEMENT

AS THE YOUTH SEE IT

Highly Favored Publishing™
BOWIE, MARYLAND

Printed in the United States of America
First Printing, 2011

Highly Favored Publishing™
3540 Crain Highway #440 / Bowie, Maryland / 20716
Highly Favored Publishing™ is an entity of Highly Favored, L.L.C.
www.highlyfavoredpublishing.com

Page 36 & Act II: pages 5-6: Reprinted by permission of the Dudley Randall Literary Estate. "Booker T. and W.E.B." in *Roses and Revolutions: The Selected Writings of Dudley Randall* (2009).

To Kiamsha

ACKNOWLEDGMENTS

Project funded by the Carl Dunn Foundation Fund.
Carl Dunn, owner and my loving, supportive husband of 42 years.

A special thanks to my father, Rev. Vernon Spencer, who first introduced me to Dr. Carter G. Woodson by housing in his library not only the *The Mis-Education of the Negro* (1933) but also Woodson's thought-provoking collection *The Journal of Negro History* (now *The Journal of African American History*), providing me the opportunity to browse through the pages of this premier journal and read this seminal work as a pre-teen. My Christian upbringing, along with Bible study and exposure to the profound words of Dr. Woodson, gave me a very mature and balanced perspective on race relations at a very young age. The research and compilation of this work is inspired totally because of Dr. Woodson's work. Thanks to the Association for the Study of African American Life and History, Inc. and its scholars and historians who continue to mentor and produce young scholars to perpetuate continuously the legacy of the Father of Black History, Dr. Woodson. Thank you for providing the truth about the history of people of African descent so they will not become a negligible factor in the thought and life of people in the global community. Thanks to the Kiamsha/ASALH family who made this project possible. A special thank you to Dr. Melvette Melvin Davis who I believe provided the timing for this project to come to fruition by finalizing her doctorate degree and establishing her publishing company just in time to publish this project. I'm forever grateful for the Kiamsha alumni who continue to keep me current in technology and give me the desire to keep providing opportunities for youth as we work jointly to develop a cadre of young people who will develop into leaders with integrity.

BEFORE AND BEYOND THE NIAGARA MOVEMENT
AS THE YOUTH SEE IT

TABLE OF CONTENTS

Growing up in a small town in the Panhandle of Texas, my discovery of my true condition was never realized until I was 30 years old. I did not realize that I would have been considered financially "poor" by economic standards because my life was so rich in every way that mattered. The youth in the African American community in Amarillo, Texas during the 1950s lived a sheltered life because the adults on my side of the tracks clearly buffered the youth from the burgeoning impact of segregation in this country. However, my mom and dad, Rev. Vernon and Novella Spencer, sheltered their three girls even more. I was never allowed to be in a situation where I had to wonder about the value of who I was as a person. Because my parents never allowed us to go downtown until we were sixteen years old (which I never understood but was just obedient to the command), I never saw the colored only/white only water fountain signs while growing up. I was never forced to sit in the balcony of a theater rather than the main floor to view a movie. I never had to go to the back door of a restaurant or go through the front door to purchase my food and leave rather than sit down to eat because of the color of my skin. I never went into a library and was told I could not check out a book or into a shoe store and told I could not try on the shoes. I remember utilizing the services of the book mobile that would come to my home so I could turn in books I had already read, then choose new ones, never knowing that I could not go to the library downtown. I never realized until years later that this resource was fought for by the adults in our community to ensure the youth had the opportunity to read beyond what was available to us in our community. Yes, my parents and my community sheltered me from all of that.

I remember viewing pictures on the television of people being hosed with water and attacked by dogs, not realizing until 2008 that those people were children who were my age at the time. I remember seeing children being escorted into schools by military force because Whites did not want them to attend. I remember my mom and dad making sure we watched President Kennedy speak on television as he verbally put an end to segregation in 1963, denouncing the visual attacks on children in Birmingham. I also remember not experiencing integration in my hometown until 1967 because of several methods of delay by the leaders in our town. I remember the day we were at school and heard that President Kennedy had been assassinated; grief and disbelief filled my heart. I remember being offered a "Freedom of Choice Agreement" in 1967 to attend one of the all-White high schools in the city but choosing to remain at our all-Black high school. I remember, in the fall of that same year, being forced to integrate. I remember watching the riots in Washington, D.C. in 1968 because Dr. King had been assassinated and seeing parts of the city burned. It was like an out of body experience because I knew what I saw was really happening, but I could not really wrap my mind around its reality.

The disconnects that I experienced, and the discovery of truth as I connected the dots over the years, are my reasons for researching and compiling this document. For several years now, I have had the opportunity to present to groups of sometimes 300 teachers, and more often than not, only one or two have ever heard the name Carter G. Woodson—and the majority have never heard of the Association for the Study of African American Life and History—many were history teachers. It is with the discovery of the large numbers of people who, like me, either have no information or misinformation that this document is provided as a resource for discovery of the true account of the history of the United States, a history that includes the experiences of African Americans.

I realize now, more than ever, that the method my parents used to raise my sisters and me had an indelible mark on who I am as an adult today. My parents provided me an opportunity to grow up knowing who I was without ever feeling inferior. My mom used to always say to us, "*If you know you have not done anything to cause someone to act negatively towards you, don't take it personal—take it as an opportunity to teach.*" I heard these words over and over and over again as a young person. So when I was sixteen and ventured into the downtown world of the city where I spent most of my childhood and had my first encounter with racism,

I took it as an opportunity to teach the young lady at the Woolworth counter who waited on six White customers ahead of me (It took me that many times to be sure she was ignoring me and my seven friends—this was shortly after Woolworth was finally integrated in our city.). My *point of reference* dictated my understanding and my reaction. Therefore, this publication is a direct result of an upbringing that provided me the opportunity to discover the importance of knowing your history and understanding who you are in history (and who you are in Christ). Because of my experiences and my upbringing, I am compelled to serve as a catalyst to affect harmony among the races throughout the global community. I believe, as Dr. Woodson did, that if people knew the rich contributions people of African descent have made to the history of this country and around the world, they would not see them as inferior.

My introduction to Dr. Carter G. Woodson as a pre-teen was a direct result of growing up in that sheltered household. My dad was a scholar of scholars. Not only was he a biblical scholar, serving as pastor of a church for 36 years and spending hours each day meditating on the Word of God, but he also studied historical books, reading almanacs from cover to cover, even studying the history of lynching in this country. I remember seeing volumes of *The Journal of Negro History* and a copy of *The Mis-Education of the Negro* right on the bookshelf of my Dad's library of books. I would often pick up the books, read through them, and sit next to my dad and ask many questions about the truth of the information in the books.

When I turned 50, in the year 2000, I received a call from the executive director of the Association for the Study of African American Life and History (ASALH), who had received my name from a mutual friend, asking me to share my resume and come in for an interview—she was in need of an administrative assistant. At this time, I was not interested in a nine to five, as I had just started a public relations firm with two of my friends three years prior. However, once I realized this was the organization that Dr. Carter G. Woodson founded in 1915 and the organization that established Negro History Week (now celebrated as Black History Month), by the time our interview was over she asked me, "How much do we need to pay you?" and I said, "Whatever you can afford."

Three significant events happened in the first two weeks of my work at ASALH. As I was looking through the office one day, thinking of ways to reorganize the work area, I saw on the shelf several copies of *The Journal of Negro History* and immediately had a déjà vu moment. These were the books that lined the shelves of my father's makeshift library. Several days later, I ran across a collection of Rev. Francis Grimke's sermons published by the Associated Publishers. My dad owned several of these volumes, as well. And last, but not least, I answered the phone one day, and on the other end was the pastor of the church where my dad had served as pastor for 36 years, whom I knew exceptionally well. When I told him who I was, we were both shocked. When he told me he was calling to order the Black History Month Kit, I asked him how he knew about these materials. Then, he told me he was just following suit, that each year, for many years, my dad had ordered the kit. I sat there astounded and speechless. *So that was where my mom got some of the unique crafts, photos, and other items that my sisters and I would use in our history and art projects.* After these events transpired, I set out to enter the mind of Dr. Woodson in a more profound way. I asked several of the historians whether Dr. Woodson was a Christian without receiving an answer that was satisfactory. So, I began to read every set of minutes written by Dr. Woodson in the early days of the Association, and I reread *The Mis-Education of the Negro*. Reading these items as an adult, I discovered the Carter G. Woodson that my dad was so enamored with. Dr. Woodson's *point of reference* dictated his understanding and caused him to sacrifice everything unselfishly to ensure his people would not become a negligible factor in the thought and life of people around the world. I believe no man's education is complete if he does not know the Bible—the most significant historical book. I discovered in Dr. Woodson's writing a significant amount of biblical knowledge and the use of a concept that I promote with the youth and adults I serve—the concept of "meeting people where they are." I knew then, without a doubt, that I had been called to do this work but did not yet know the fullness of this call.

When I began my work in August of 2000, my first assignment was to organize the Youth Day for the 2000 ASALH Conference that was held in Washington, D.C. By now, I had discovered that the average age of the members in this 85-year-old organization was over 65 years old. I realized then that Youth Day needed to be a transformative effort. Since I had been serving since 1993 as executive director of a youth empowerment organization that used history to help cultivate communications skills for youth, I presented the idea to ASALH to use these youth to facilitate Youth Day for the 2000 convention. The rest is history. In 2000, Kiamsha Youth Empowerment Organization joined forces with ASALH as partners, and Kiamsha has facilitated Youth Day ever since that time.

By 2005, five years after beginning my journey with ASALH, I had begun to see the reason why I was there. One, to infuse a cadre of youth into the workings of this organization in order to ensure continuation of the Woodson legacy, and two, to help my generation, the Baby Boomers, and my elders in the Silent and Greatest Generations, feel comfortable passing the torch to the next generation. This publication is a direct result of my personal understanding of how many people, not only the youth, who have not personally lived the history, but also the many adults who lived but did not examine further historical facts and connect the dots for their own understanding.

The accompanying script is written in the voice of four high school students who are portrayed by youth from the Kiamsha Youth Empowerment Organization. In the script, the students have just discovered that African American history has been infused throughout their school curriculum, and using factual information, they analyze events and decisions made by their ancestors. Using the Niagara Movement as the central theme, a project assigned by their teacher helps them connect the dots before and after this significant, lesser-known, historical movement.

We are living in tumultuous times. I challenge you to use this document as a guide to discover why history is key to bringing people together in harmony. Dr. Woodson's words of wisdom are used as a "voice of reason" throughout this project, and his work, *The Mis-Education of the Negro* (1933), is compelling when we look at it in light of what is happening in our world today. Throughout Dr. Woodson's scholarship and leadership, he emphasized that thinking was critical to progress. In *The Mis-Education* he contends, "The Association for the Study of Negro Life and History has no set solution to the problem of race except to learn to think" (p.108). He explains that "When you control a man's thinking, you don't have to worry about his actions" (p. xiii). He also advises us that "the mere imparting of information is not education. The effort must result in making a man think and do for himself" (p. xii). Without truth to guide our thoughts, there are many whose hearts will remain filled with garbage planted by untruths and the ignorance that keeps one from discovering truth. As the Word of God says in Matthew 12:34b, "Out of the abundance of the heart the mouth speaks." I have now discovered the fullness of being planted to serve ASALH. My mission in life has collided with Dr. Woodson's mission—to promote harmony among the races to accomplish the cause of Christ, which is brotherhood among mankind using the same method that Jesus used during his time on earth—the method of "meeting people where they are."

It is my hope that after venturing out to use this document as a guide to teach, or even to pursue personal study, you will recall many of the untruths you may have been taught or passed on to others and take personal responsibility to re-parent and re-educate yourself so we can come together with a clarion call to help make this world a better place to live for all people. This is a call to re-educate "we the people," and this document is a resource dedicated to the youth of Kiamsha as a means for them to continue to perpetuate the legacy of Dr. Carter Godwin Woodson, who is not only the Father of Black History but also a pioneer of multiculturalism. *Enjoy your journey.*

INTRODUCTION

The educational DVD and curriculum guide are resources designed to help teachers, advisors, mentors, and parents lead students through activities that take a critical look at the history of people of African descent in an effort to help students incorporate these facts into their knowledge of United States history. By exploring these missing pieces of United States history that have largely been ignored in the textbooks, we hope that all who engage in this educational project will come to a better understanding of their individual "points of reference" and help move the discussion of slavery to a productive place in the United States and around the world.

Leaders will guide students through the objectives underlining the educational DVD and curriculum guide and encourage students to keep these objectives in mind as they progress through each lesson's activities. The lessons encourage students to analyze and critique the actions of historical leaders featured throughout the DVD and curriculum. Our ultimate goal is to challenge students to devise a plan of action that will endeavor to change how people, especially those in the United States, will interact 20 years from the release of this DVD, as it relates to racial harmony.

There are six main components to the first five lessons: (1) GOALS, (2) ACTIVITIES, (3) KIAMSHA'S DID YOU KNOW?, (4) KIAMSHA CONCEPT, (5) KEY TERMS, and (6) HOW MUCH DO YOU REMEMBER?. The KIAMSHA CONCEPT section serves as a character-building tool for students as they engage in learning their history as we strive through this curriculum to cultivate leaders of integrity. The KIAMSHA DID YOU KNOW? section provides additional facts about African American history and serves as a critical thinking exercise that will hopefully further students' interest in the topic presented and promote self-reflection and behavior changes. *Always review this section in advance.*

The sixth lesson features components one, two, and five and also includes several activities that focus on character building and helping students devise a plan for making the world a better place.

We used Dr. Woodson's quote, "The Association for the Study of Negro Life and History has no set solution to the problem of race except to learn to think," as a framework for this project (p. 108). Teaching young people how to think critically is our goal, and we believe that a thinking people need truth to guide their thoughts. With this educational DVD, we aim to provide "truth" about the history of people of African descent, especially African Americans, in order to help students engage in discussions with as much factual information as possible so they can make informed decisions.

Included on the Kiamsha Youth Empowerment Organization website (kiamshayouth.org) are several resources related to the DVD and curriculum, including a teambuilding exercise that highlights Dr. Woodson's early life experiences. The exercise is intended to introduce Dr. Woodson as a young boy who grew up in poverty, yet, because of his self-knowledge, he became the second African American (W.E.B. DuBois was the first) to receive his Ph.D. from the prestigious Harvard University during the nadir of race relations in the United States of America. Also included on our site is a resource entitled "Talking Points for a Scholarly Conversation," which is guided by the questions, "What is holding us stagnant?" "What is blocking our path?" Click on the Curriculum Resources tab on the kiamshayouth.org website for more tools and information.

With this DVD and curriculum, it is my hope that teachers who really want to move the conversation of race in America forward, as well as leaders who want to see all children excel and succeed academically, will take the time to review and internalize these tools and also utilize them to challenge others to seek the truth.

The Association for the Study of African American Life and History, its publications, and interviews of its scholars and historians were the primary sources used to write the script for the DVD and the accompanying curriculum guide. The DVD features a production performed by youth and young adults who discussed history from their perspective using their research, knowledge, and understanding of the past. The script used for the DVD is included in this guide because we challenge young people not only to view the DVD but also to engage thoughtfully in discussions about the information presented and reenact the script in their own way in their schools and communities. The play is comprised of six acts, and the six lessons included in the guide correspond with each act of the play. Each lesson's activities also provide an opportunity to analyze and explore words from Dr. Woodson during his leadership of the association until his death, from 1915 to 1950, in an effort to help young people understand why Dr. Woodson operated as he did as leader of the association. His focus and work ethic provide an impeccable example for youth engaging in this project. ENJOY!

References

Woodson, C. G. (2005). *The Mis-Education of the Negro*. Washington, DC: The ASALH Press. (Reprinted from 1933)

Lesson ONE

Introduction: Understanding the Past

GOALS:

1) Students will review the objectives underlining the educational DVD and curriculum guide.

2) Students will compare Kiamsha's slavery timeline with a timeline of at least one country on the continent of Africa that surveys the same time period. Students will refer to the timelines throughout the six lessons.

ACTIVITY ONE:

▶ Distribute and discuss overall objectives with students. (pg. 20)

OBJECTIVES

1) Students will research the elements of a democratic society as defined by the Niagara Movement and the "Declaration of Principles" manifesto.

2) Students will compare and contrast the rights and liberties they experience in their own lives with the rights and liberties the Niagara Movement men and women were fighting for.

3) Students will research the origin and use of the "N" word and devise a plan to motivate people in society, especially their own generation, to eliminate it from their vocabulary.

4) Beginning with 1619, students will plot a timeline of landmarks/events significant to African descended American citizens in the United States. Using the same beginning year, students will create a timeline that displays landmarks/events significant to citizens of African descent on at least one country on the continent of Africa. Students will compare events on these timelines in an effort to answer the question, "Why enslavement?"
   INSTRUCTIONAL STRATEGY: Teachers should use the Internet to set up a virtual collaboration with a class in an African country. This activity will stimulate dialogue with students from an African country and help students gain accurate information for the historical timeline.

5) Students will define and identify examples of colonialism.
   INSTRUCTIONAL STRATEGY: Use *How Europe Underdeveloped Africa* (1981) by Walter Rodney as an informational guide. Have students research Walter Rodney's life story.

6) Students will research and examine the relationships between people of African descent and other ethnic groups throughout the world.

7) Students will research inventions made in the United States of America by people of African descent.

8) Students will explore the implications of ethnocentrism and the inferiority and superiority concepts they perpetuate.

9) By the end of this unit, students will be able to describe the differences between "United States history" and "American history."

10) Students will begin creating a plan to positively impact history for future generations in an effort to leave the world in better shape than it is in the present, especially as it relates to racial harmony. Students will finalize this plan of action after the sixth lesson, when all activities have been completed. Students should revisit their plan yearly.

ACTIVITY TWO:

▶ Distribute and review with students "Kiamsha Concept: S.T.A.R." (pg. 25).

   INSTRUCTIONAL STRATEGY: Brainstorm/conduct an activity for your students that will emphasize the Kiamsha Concept.

▶ Distribute and review with students "Key Terms" (pg. 26).

▶ Review with students "Kiamsha's Did You Know?" trivia (pg. 24).

ACTIVITY THREE:

▶ Have students view "Chapter One" on the DVD, and have students list all the personalities reflected in the images shown throughout this segment.

▶ Organize students into groups of four, and have each group research and identify the following:

1) Name
2) Birth date
3) Ethnic Background
4) What generation was this person born into?
5) What was the person's contribution(s) to society?
6) What was the person's philosophy/what did they believe?
7) What accomplishment(s) make this person most notable?

▶ Distribute "Woodson Quotes" handout (pg. 19) to students, and have students analyze the meaning behind each quote. Have students discuss in their groups the significance of Dr. Woodson's quotes in today's society.

ACTIVITY FOUR:

▶ Turn the lights out in the room, and play the following songs on the *Pathways* CD: "Love Ye One Another," "Rainbow of Love," and "Pathways."

▶ Discuss with students the lyrics to each song using the following prompts as a guide: *What is the theme expressed in each song. Is there a message you think would be useful today? If yes, share with your group the message you think is applicable to our society today.*

▶ Have students take note of how long it took for their eyes to adjust to the dark room once the lights were turned out. (This realization will be discussed later in the activities in Lesson Two: Activity Seven (pg. 32).)

ACTIVITY FIVE:

▶ Review with students the "Slavery Timeline" on pages 22-23. Have students work together in groups of four to plot their own timeline of landmarks/events significant to African descended American citizens in the United States, beginning in the year 1619. Then, using the same beginning year, have groups create a timeline that displays landmarks/events significant to citizens of African descent on at least one country on the continent of Africa. Use the "Some Countries in Africa and the Americas" handout on page 21 to help students choose a country to explore. Students will compare events on these timelines in an effort to answer the question, "Why enslavement?"

ACTIVITY SIX:

▶ Quiz students with "How Much Do You Remember" trivia (pg. 27).

Lesson ONE

HANDOUTS AND MATERIALS

WOODSON QUOTES

Lesson One: Understanding the Past

"In ancient days, men had less race hate than we find today. The earliest historians recorded the achievements of all nations regardless of race or color. Even in the case of little contact, there was an effort to give honorable mention to all. Homer, for example, mentioned the Ethiopians as the "farthest removed of men." Herodotus said the Ethiopians feasted among the gods. As kingdoms and empires developed around powerful dynasties, however, history tended to become self-glorification and an inculcation of national bias, race hate, and race prejudice. In the modern world we are the heirs of this incubus. Teachers of history, then, have been largely propagandists selecting those truths which stimulate these vicious tendencies and rejecting those which work to the contrary. The schools of America and Europe, therefore, have practically no conception of history. They have been so far misled by propaganda that actual history is branded as heresy" (p. 25).

"If we would know history, we must not tarry too long with the exploits of Alexander the Great, the campaigns of Caesar, or the conquests of Napoleon. Warriors deserve attention as regimes to clear the way for the new, but these military chieftains were not intentionally great men. They aspired to be imposters, exploiters, and oppressors, rather than benefactors of humanity. We should record the achievements of men like Watts with the steam engine, Fulton with the steamboat, Morse with the telegraph, Bell with the telephone, Marconi with the wireless telegraph, Roentgen with the X-ray, Edison with the phonograph, and Matzliger with the lasting machine by which the shoe industry was revolutionized. We should exalt Socrates dying for the truth among the Greeks, St. Francis Assisi giving up all to help the poor, and Savonarola presenting himself as a living sacrifice for the faith. And we must not forget such reformers as Woolman, Benezet, Jefferson, Wilberforce, Cobden, Bright, Phillips, Douglas [sic], Garrison, Sumner, Lovejoy, and Lincoln, who have illuminated the pages of modern history" (p. 25).

Woodson, C.G. (2002). Observances of Negro History Week. *Black History Bulletin, 65,* 1-35.

OBJECTIVES
Before and Beyond The Niagara Movement—
As the Youth See It

1) Students will research the elements of a democratic society as defined by the Niagara Movement and the "Declaration of Principles" manifesto.

2) Students will compare and contrast the rights and liberties they experience in their own lives with the rights and liberties the Niagara Movement men and women were fighting for.

3) Students will research the origin and use of the "N" word and devise a plan to motivate people in society, especially their own generation, to eliminate it from their vocabulary.

4) Beginning with 1619, students will plot a timeline of landmarks/events significant to African descended American citizens in the United States. Using the same beginning year, students will create a timeline that displays landmarks/events significant to citizens of African descent on at least one country on the continent of Africa. Students will compare events on these timelines in an effort to answer the question, "Why enslavement?"

5) Students will define and identify examples of colonialism.

6) Students will research and examine the relationships between people of African descent and other ethnic groups throughout the world.

7) Students will research inventions made in the United States of America by people of African descent.

8) Students will explore the implications of ethnocentrism and the inferiority and superiority concepts they perpetuate.

9) By the end of this unit, students will be able to describe the differences between "United States history" and "American history."

10) Students will begin creating a plan to positively impact history for future generations in an effort to leave the world in better shape than it is in the present, especially as it relates to racial harmony. Students should revisit their list yearly.

SOME COUNTRIES IN AFRICA AND THE AMERICAS

1. Haiti
2. Brazil
3. Jamaica
4. Senegal
5. Sierra Leone
6. Liberia
7. Ivory Coast
8. Ghana
9. Nigeria
10. Cameroon
11. Gabon
12. Congo
13. Gambia
14. Guinea-Bissau
15. Togo
16. Benin
17. Angola
18. Mozambique
19. Cuba
20. Mexico
21. Barbados

SLAVERY TIMELINE

1526   The first group of Africans to set foot on what is now the United States is brought by a Spanish explorer to establish a settlement in South Carolina. However, the group escapes to the interior and settles with Native Americans.

1565   African slaves arrive on North American mainland at Spanish colony of St. Augustine.

1619   The origin of slavery in English colonies began with the arrival of 20 Africans to Jamestown, Virginia.

1641   Colony of Massachusetts Bay legalizes slavery.

1660   Virginia legalizes slavery.

1760s   Charles Mason and Jeremiah Dixon survey Pennsylvania/Maryland boundary; in time, this marks the division between *slave states* and *free states*.

1770   Crispus Attucks is killed by British soldiers in the Boston Massacre.

1775   First abolition society forms in Philadelphia.

1776   Delegates of Continental Congress in Philadelphia adopt the Declaration of Independence on July 4.

1787   The states draft the U.S. Constitution, which forbids Congress from interfering with the slave trade before 1808. Enslaved persons are counted as three-fifths of a person for the census.

1793   The U.S. Congress enacts the Fugitive Slave Act to protect the rights of slave owners retrieving runaways.

1803   Haitians achieve independence from France after a 13-year rebellion, and they abolish slavery.

1817   Andrew Jackson takes command of federal troops engaging in a ruthless war against Seminoles and runaways in Florida.

1820-1821   Missouri Compromise admits Missouri and Maine into the Union to maintain the balance of the slave and free states; Missouri Compromise also establishes line between free and slave territory.

1830s   Vigilance committees organize in Northern cities to prevent return of fugitive slaves to the South.

1831   William Lloyd Garrison begins publication of the abolitionist newspaper *The Liberator*.

1831   Nat Turner leads slave insurrection in Virginia.

1833   William Lloyd Garrison heads New England Anti-Slavery Society; Margaretta Forten forms Female Anti-slavery Society in Philadelphia; British Parliament passes Emancipation Act freeing all slaves and outlawing the slave trade.

1838   Black abolitionist Robert Purvis becomes chairman of the General Vigilance Committee. This Committee's task was to assist runaways in New York City.

1839   Slaves revolt on Spanish ship Amistad near Cuba.

1847   Frederick Douglass begins publication of his abolitionist newspaper *The North Star*.

1848   First Women's Rights Convention held in Seneca Falls, New York; abolitionists Lucretia Mott, Elizabeth Cady Stanton, and Frederick Douglass attend.

1848   Seventy-seven enslaved people in Washington, D.C. made a risky bid for freedom on April 15, 1848 when they attempted to escape on the Pearl, a 54-ton, bay-craft schooner on the Potomac River waterway.

1852   Harriet Beecher Stowe's *Uncle Tom's Cabin* is published.

1854   Black abolitionist Frances Ellen Watkins Harper is hired by Maine Anti-slavery Society to lecture in New England and Lower Canada.

1854   Kansas-Nebraska Act allows territories to choose to be slave or free states.

1857   U.S. Supreme Court's Dred Scott Decision rules that free blacks and slaves are not citizens.

1859   Abolitionist John Brown raids U.S. Armory at Harpers Ferry.

1860   Republican Abraham Lincoln wins U.S. Presidential election in November; South Carolina secedes from Union in December.

1861   Civil War begins as Confederates attack Fort Sumter in April; Union declares fugitive slaves as contraband of war in May.

1862   In March, Congress abolishes slavery in District of Columbia and provides funds for voluntary colonizations; In May, Congress prohibits slavery in territories; In July, the Second Confiscation Act permits military to enlist blacks.

1863   The Emancipation Proclamation becomes effective January 1, 1863. President Abraham Lincoln's action made abolition of slavery as important a goal in the prosecution of the Civil War as preserving the Federal Union; Union intensifies recruitment of blacks as soldiers.

1865   Civil War ends; Lincoln assassinated; The Thirteenth amendment, which abolishes slavery (except when you commit a crime), is ratified by the required three-fourths of the states on December 18.

Ft. Mose, located in a salt marsh north of
St. Augustine, Florida, is the first Black Settlement
in the Northern American colonies?

For more information, visit
http://www.archaeology.org/9609/abstracts/ftmose.html

TRIVIA

What is this settlement's relationship to the
Underground Railroad?

KIAMSHA CONCEPT:
S.T.A.R.

STOP and give yourself time to think

THINK about all the options, deciding what is best based on the qualities of life and factual information that you personally know

ACT on what you have decided, and

REVIEW your decision. It is a lot easier to appreciate a well thought-out decision after the fact

STOP and THINK!

KEY TERMS

Modern-Day Underground Railroad Concept – Reveals the fact that during the Enslavement era, there were no slaves but people who were *enslaved* by their slave masters. However, youth and adults today have become *slaves* to the modern-day slave masters known as alcohol and other drugs, premarital sexual activity, violence, racial disharmony, jealousy, envy, and the list goes on. Kiamsha challenges you to use the same level of conviction the enslaved people used in the Enslavement era—they did whatever it took to free themselves from the slave master. They even walked miles in unhealthy and tiring conditions

Slave – Someone who willingly gives up their freedom to someone or something

Enslaved – To have one's freedom taken away against her or his will

Self-Determination – The right of a people to choose their own destiny

Culture – The totality of socially transmitted behavior patterns, arts, beliefs, institutions, and all other products of human work and thought typical of a population or community at a given time. Example: Teenagers are a culture

Conviction – A basic moral principle that you purpose to follow no matter what the costs. Convictions never change

Preference – A decision that changes from situation to situation

Point of Choice – The exact moment when a decision is made that results in a point in time when you cannot go back, usually resulting in placing a person in a compromising situation

Innate – Possessed at birth
Example: Everyone was born with the innate ability to discern right from wrong

Character – The combination of emotional, intellectual, and moral qualities distinguishing one person from another; distinctive feature or attribute; moral or ethical strength; INTEGRITY

Qualities of life – Character traits that can only be developed with the help of the Spirit within you. The Spirit produces these character traits, and we cannot obtain them by trying to get them by ourselves. Growth is gradual; man can assist producing it but cannot initiate it or assure its production. By obtaining all of these character traits, we can fulfill our intended purpose. The qualities are *love, joy, peace, longsuffering, gentleness, goodness (kindness), faithfulness, and self-control*

Integrity – Doing the right thing even when no one is looking

REMEMBER?

1) **NAME** FOUR PERSONALITIES YOU WERE INTRODUCED TO IN THIS LESSON AND WHAT THEY WILL BE MOST REMEMBERED FOR.

2) **ACCORDING** TO THE SLAVERY TIMELINE, WHAT YEAR DID THE FIRST GROUP OF AFRICANS SET FOOT ON WHAT IS KNOWN AS THE UNITED STATES?

3) **SHARE** ONE OF THE COMPARISONS AND A CONTRAST THAT YOU DISCOVERED WHILE STUDYING THE TIMELINES FOR THE UNITED STATES AND THE COUNTRY YOU CHOSE IN AFRICA.

4) **SHARE** WHAT YOU BELIEVE IS THE MOST SIGNIFICANT QUOTE BY DR. WOODSON IN THIS SEGMENT AND EXPLAIN WHY.

Lesson TWO

The Niagara Movement

Lesson TWO

GOAL:

Students will study the key founders of the Niagara Movement, W.E.B. DuBois and William Monroe Trotter, and the ascendancy of the man this movement directly challenged, Booker T. Washington.

ACTIVITY ONE:

▶ Review with students "Objectives" from Lesson One (pg. 20).

▶ Distribute and review with students "Kiamsha Concept: Understanding Your Thought Process" (pg. 39).

   INSTRUCTIONAL STRATEGY: Brainstorm/conduct an activity for your students that will emphasize this Kiamsha Concept.

▶ Distribute and review with students "Key Terms" (pg. 40).

▶ Review with students "Kiamsha's Did You Know?" trivia (pg. 38).

ACTIVITY TWO:

▶ Have students view "Chapter Two" on the DVD. As they watch the film, have students record all historical facts discussed in the students' dialogue on the DVD. Have students discuss as a class the facts they learned.

▶ Have students recall the "It Seems to Me" dialogue they recently viewed on the DVD and have them discuss and decide which personality, between DuBois or Washington, stated all the "It seems to me" statements and which personality stated all the "I don't agree?" statements.

▶ Distribute the poem "Booker T. and W.E.B." (1969) by Dudley Randall (pg. 36). Have students write a creative response that characterizes DuBois' and Washington's philosophies. They may draw on the monologue depictions or other historical information about them they have learned. The response can be a rap, poem, an essay, a dialogue, etc. Whatever the student chooses.

ACTIVITY THREE:

▶ Review with students the "Declaration of Principles," (pg. 37) and have students write an essay discussing the relevance of the principles to their lives today.

ACTIVITY FOUR:

▶ Distribute "Woodson Quotes" handout (pg. 35) and have students write the meaning of the quote(s) in their own words. Encourage students to use a dictionary to write down definitions of words they do not understand. Have students share their interpretations with the class.

ACTIVITY FIVE:

▶ Organize students into groups of four, and have each group list all the people mentioned in the "Woodson Quote" for this DVD segment. Have groups research and identify the following:

1) Name
2) Birth date
3) Ethnic Background
4) What generation was this person born into?

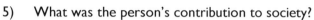

5) What was the person's contribution to society?
6) What was the person's philosophy/what did they believe?
7) For what accomplishment is this person most remembered?

ACTIVITY Six:

▶ Have students come to class dressed in the character of one of the persons discussed in this lesson. For the entire class session, have the students portray the character of the person they are dressed as, never breaking character. Students will have to research thoroughly how the person thought, and they should respond to everything during the class session as though they were that character.

ACTIVITY Seven:

▶ Have students reflect back to Lesson One when they listened to the three songs with the lights out. Ask them to consider the following: *How long does it take to be in darkness before you can easily walk in darkness without regard for it?* Connect for students this analogy to the S.I.N. concept (pgs. 38 & 40). **THINK ABOUT IT!**

ACTIVITY Eight:

▶ Have students choose a significant event they learned from this lesson to plot on their timeline.
▶ Quiz students with "How Much Do You Remember" trivia (pg. 41).

Lesson TWO

HANDOUTS AND MATERIALS

WOODSON QUOTES

Lesson Two: The Niagara Movement

"We should especially emphasize the virtues of the heroes and heroines who, imbibing the spirit of the Great Nazarene, have suffered and died for ideals. As He died to make men holy, they call the roll of Daniel Drayton in the jail of the capital of the nation, L.W. Paine in the State prison in Georgia, Calvin Fairbank twice under such a sentence in Kentucky, and Andrew Torrey dying in the Maryland penitentiary, all merely because they helped the fugitive on the way to freedom. Among them we should give a high place of honor to Nat Turner who lived up to the ideal of Jesus that, "greater love hath no man than this, that a man lay down his life for his friends." And John Brown, inspired by the example of Nat Turner, would close the chapter with the moral courage and martyrdom, which made him one of the saints of God" (p. 28).

Woodson, C.G. (2002). Observances of Negro History Week. *Black History Bulletin, 65,* 1-35.

Booker T. and W.E.B. (1969)
Dudley Randall

"It seems to me," said Booker T.,
"It shows a mighty lot of cheek
To study chemistry and Greek
When Mister Charlie needs a hand
To hoe the cotton on his land,
And when Miss Ann looks for a cook,
Why stick your nose inside a book?"

"I don't agree," said W.E.B.,
"If I should have the drive to seek
Knowledge of chemistry or Greek,
I'll do it. Charles and Miss can look
Another place for hand or cook.
Some men rejoice in skill of hand,
And some in cultivating land,
But there are others who maintain
The right to cultivate the brain."

"It seems to me," said Booker T.,
"That all you folks have missed the boat
Who shout about the right to vote,
And spend vain days and sleepless nights
In uproar over civil rights.
Just keep your mouths shut, do not grouse,
But work, and save, and buy a house."

"I don't agree," said W.E.B.,
"For what can property avail
If dignity and justice fail.
Unless you help to make the laws,
They'll steal your house with trumped-up clause.
A rope's as tight, a fire as hot,
No matter how much cash you've got.
Speak soft, and try your little plan,
But as for me, I'll be a man."

"It seems to me," said Booker T.—
"I don't agree,"
Said W.E.B.

Declaration of Principles (1905)
W.E.B. DuBois and Willam Monroe Trotter

Number one, freedom of speech and criticism. Number two, an unfettered and unsubsidized press. We suggest that the press is bought and controlled and contend that we would remain a captive race unless our own propaganda reaches and arouses the people. Number three, manhood suffrage. We demand to participate in the American political system, North and South, on the same basis as whites. Number four, the abolition of all caste distinctions based simply on race and color. Racism was denounced as "unreasoning human savagery" and Jim Crow was condemned as an avenue for insult as well as "crucifixion of manhood." Number five, the recognition of the principles of human brotherhood as a practical present creed. DuBois considered that the Niagara Movement's task was to interpret the real Christ to white Christians. Number six, recognition of the highest and best human training is a monopoly of no class or race. The Niagara men believed in universal common school education. High school and technical high school were to be available to those "who wanted them." Number seven, a belief in the dignity of labor.

KIAMSHA'S
DID YOU KNOW?

S.I.N. will take you further than you meant to be taken, keep you longer than you wanted to stay, and cost you more than you were planning to pay!! It is not **S.I.N.** to be tempted. It does not become **S.I.N.** until you yield to the temptation in thought or in outward action!

Did you know you should never call someone stupid (pg. 40)? Only you can be the judge of your own stupidity because you really do not know whether or not another person has all the information necessary to make a right choice. Age alone is not the judge for knowledge. But you can judge yourself . . .

YOU do KNOW what you KNOW!

DID YOU KNOW THAT YOUR THOUGHTS COME FROM THREE SOURCES?
THEY COME FROM . . .

GOOD   EVIL   SELF

DID YOU KNOW THAT YOUR MIND IS A
BATTLEGROUND?

KIAMSHA CONCEPT:
Understanding Your Thought Process

THREE STEPS TO THE BIRTH OF S.I.N.

1. **CONCEPTION** – When the thought enters your mind

2. **GESTATION** – When you plan the idea in your mind. You actually commit the S.I.N. in thought!

3. **BIRTH** – S.I.N. is born when the thought becomes an outward ACTION

KEY TERMS

Ascendancy – Movement upward; to rise; domination

Dominate – To influence, control, or rule by superior power or authority

Philosophy – Inquiry into the nature of things based on logical reasoning rather than empirical methods

Empirical – Capable of verification by means of experimentation or observation

Principle – A basic truth, law, or assumption; a rule or standard, especially moral or ethical standards or judgments

Moral – Concerned with the principles of right and wrong

Ethical – Conforming to accepted principles of right and wrong that govern the conduct of a profession or society

Point of Reference – The origin of a person's beliefs and values, usually gained from influences derived from their orientation family or environment

S.I.N. – Self-inflicted nonsense. You bring the consequences of **S.I.N.** on yourself by the choices you make, and it's just plain stupid!

Nonsense – A decision made without regard to factual information or with no regard for the affect the decision will have on you or others; a stupid decision

Stupid – When you **KNOW** all the information necessary to make the right decision, but **CHOOSE** to do **ANYWAY** what you **INNATELY KNOW** is the wrong thing to do

Ignorant – You just don't know!

How Much Do You REMEMBER?

1) **WHAT** IS THE NAME OF MONROE TROTTER'S NEWSPAPER THAT PLAYED A SIGNIFICANT ROLE IN ENERGIZING DUBOIS, THE NIAGARA MOVEMENT, AND OTHER ANTI-WASHINGTON FORCES?

2) **HOW** MANY MEN ANSWERED W.E. B. DU BOIS' CALL TO ATTEND THE NIAGARA MOVEMENT MEETING IN BUFFALO IN 1905?

3) **OF** THAT NUMBER OF MEN, HOW MANY ACTUALLY ATTENDED THE MEETING AND HOW MANY STATES DID THEY REPRESENT?

4) **NAME** AT LEAST THREE OF THE DECLARATION OF PRINCIPLES WRITTEN BY DUBOIS AND TROTTER.

5) **ACCORDING** TO MARCUS GARVEY'S SPEECH IN THIS SEGMENT, WHAT WAS HIS REASON FOR COMING TO THE UNITED STATES? WHAT WAS THE NAME OF THE ORGANIZATION HE STARTED WHEN HE ARRIVED IN THE UNITED STATES?

Lesson THREE

Social Change

GOAL:

Students will analyze and describe social changes in the United States from 1860–1910. Students will analyze the Civil War, especially, and compare/contrast social changes during and after the war.

ACTIVITY ONE:

▶ Distribute and review with students "Kiamsha Concept: Conviction and Preference" (pg. 51).

INSTRUCTIONAL STRATEGY: Brainstorm and conduct an activity for your students that will emphasize this Kiamsha Concept.

▶ Distribute and review with students "Key Terms" (pg. 52).

▶ Review with students "Kiamsha's Did You Know?" trivia (pg. 50).

INSTRUCTIONAL STRATEGY: Assign students a project to research the presidents from Washington to Lincoln and study their policies toward the Negro. A good reference: *The Presidents and the Negro* (1982) by Romeo B. Garrett.

ACTIVITY TWO:

▶ Have students view "Chapter Three" on the DVD. As they watch the film, have students record all historical facts discussed in the students' dialogue on the DVD. Have students discuss as a class the facts they learned.

ACTIVITY THREE:

▶ Show the film "The Great Debaters" (2007). Organize students into debate teams. Assign teams one of the topics below, and assign students roles on the teams. Hold mock debates for these topics. Have students use the bullets as starting points for research.

1) **Debate topic: The Civil War was fought to end slavery.**
   a) Compare and contrast the philosophy of the North and South in the time period preceding the Civil War (1850s – 1860)
   b) What political parties existed at the time of the Civil War began.
   c) In the 1850s, discuss the Northern states promotion of prohibiting slavery in the Western territories that would eventually become new states.
   d) Analyze why the South succeeded from the Union.

2) **Debate topic: The Emancipation Proclamation freed the enslaved.**
   a) Review the Emancipation Proclamation
   b) Study at least two of President Abraham Lincoln's speeches relative to the Emancipation Proclamation.
   c) Devise a logical reason for Lincoln's signing of the Emancipation Proclamation based on historical fact only.

3) **Debate topic: Post Civil-War Black Codes were just.**
   a) Record timeframe that these codes were written.
   b) Analyze the reason for the writing of these codes.

c) Record some historical events that took place during this timeframe.

d) Describe why you think these events may have played a part in encouraging the writing of these codes.

4) **Debate topic: Social justice movements like The Niagara Movement were necessary during the Post-Civil War fight for racial equality.**
   a) Record timeframe that this organization began.
   b) Analyze the mission of the organization.
   c) Record some historical events that took place during this timeframe.
   d) Describe why you think these events may have played a part in motivating the founders of this organization and others like it.

5) **Debate topic: The Ku Klux Klan's (KKK) approach to social justice was cowardly.**
   a) Record timeframe that this organization began.
   b) Analyze the mission of this organization.
   c) Record some historical events that took place during this timeframe.
   d) Describe why you think these events may have played a part in encouraging the founders to establish the organization.

6) **Debate topic: The establisment of the NAACP was unnecessary**.
   a) Record timeframe that this organization began.
   b) Analyze the mission of this organization.
   c) Record some historical events that took place during this timeframe.
   d) Describe why you think these events may have played a part in encouraging the founder to establish the organization.

7) **Debate topic: Do we still need Black History Month?**
   a) Record timeframe during which the Association for the Study of Negro Life and History began.
   b) Analyze the mission of this organization.
   c) Record some historical events that took place during this timeframe.
   d) Describe why you think these events may have played a part in encouraging the founders to establish the organization.
   e) Research why Dr. Carter G. Woodson initiated Negro History Week.

ACTIVITY FOUR:

▶ Distribute "Woodson Quotes" handout (pg. 49) and have students write the meaning of the quote(s) in their own words. Have students share their interpretations with the class.

ACTIVITY FIVE:

▶ Have students choose a significant event they learned from this lesson to plot on their timeline.

▶ Quiz students with "How Much Do You Remember" trivia (pg. 53).

Lesson THREE

HANDOUTS AND MATERIALS

WOODSON QUOTES

Lesson Three: Social Change

"This is the meaning of Negro History Week. It is not so much a Negro History Week as it is a History Week. We should emphasize not Negro History, but the Negro in history. What we need is not history of selected races or nations, but the history of the world void of national bias, race hate, and religious prejudice. There should be no indulgence in undue eulogy of the Negro. The case of the Negro is well taken care of when it is shown how he has influenced the development of civilization" (p. 25)

The fact is, however, that one race has not accomplished any more good than any other race, for God could not be just and at the same time make one race the inferior of the other. But if you leave it to the one to set forth his own virtues while disparaging those of others, it will not require many generations before all credit for human achievements will be ascribed to one particular stock. Such is the history taught the youth today" (p. 25).

Woodson, C.G. (2002). Observances of Negro History Week. *Black History Bulletin*, 65, 1-35.

Did you know that several presidents were in favor of deportation of African Americans back to Africa?

KIAMSHA CONCEPT:
CONVICTION AND PREFERENCE

Conviction – A basic moral principle that you purpose to follow no matter what it costs you; convictions never change

Preference – A decision or choice that changes from situation to situation

KEY TERMS

Social Change
   a) Change in the nature, social structure, social behavior, social relations, or the social institutions of a society or community of people
   b) When behavior pattern changes in large numbers and is visible and sustained, it results in a social change. Once there is a divergence from culturally inherited values, it may result in a rebellion against the established system, causing a change in the social order
   c) Any event or action that affects a group of individuals who have shared values or characteristics
   d) Acts of advocacy for the cause of influencing society in a normative way (subjective).

Analyze – To consider in detail in order to discover essential features or meanings; to examine

Black Codes – Laws developed in Southern states during 1865 and 1866 to control and to inhibit the freedom of newly emancipated Blacks in the U.S. With these laws, Whites attempted to maintain the way of life they had prior to the Civil War

Emancipation – Freedom from the control of another

Organize – To put together in an orderly, functional, and structured manner

African American – A person of African descent who was born in the United States of America

Black – A person of color residing in any location throughout the world

Diaspora – A dispersion of an original, homogeneous people; a migration
Example: The body of Jews or Jewish communities settled outside Palestine or modern Israel.
Example: African Americans living outside the African continent.

1) *HOW* DID BLACK CODES AFFECT THE NEWLY FREED ENSLAVED?

2) *NAME* AT LEAST THREE ORGANIZATIONS FORMED BETWEEN 1865 – 1920 AND RECORD THE ORGANIZATIONS MISSIONS.

3) *WHY* DID LINCOLN SIGN THE EMANCIPATION PROCLAMATION?

Lesson FOUR
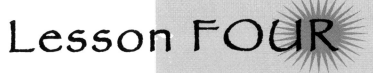

Education and Reform

Lesson FOUR

GOAL:

Students will study and describe the birth of Jim Crow, Plessy v. Ferguson, and the emergence of the NAACP and other major efforts to reform American society during the Post Civil-War era through 1910.

ACTIVITY ONE:

▶ Distribute and review with students "Kiamsha Concept: Slave vs. Enslaved" (pg. 65).
INSTRUCTIONAL STRATEGY: Have students work in groups of four to complete the "Slave vs. Enslaved" exercise on page 49. Have groups discuss their answers with the class.

▶ Distribute and review with students "Key Terms" (pg. 66).

▶ Review with students "Kiamsha's Did You Know?" trivia (pg. 64).

ACTIVITY TWO:

▶ Have students view "Chapter Four" on the DVD. As they watch the film, have students record all historical facts discussed in the students' dialogue on the DVD. Have students discuss as a class the facts they learned.

▶ Have students study Plessy v. Ferguson and discuss its negative affect in the lives of African Americans in the United States. What affect did this decision have on American reform?

▶ Use the following prompts to stimulate a class discussion:
  • African American youth are 35% of the population but 65% of the prison population.
  • African Americans are 13% of the population in the United States, but 67% of the prison population along with their Native American and Hispanic counterparts.
  • Why is there an achievement gap between White youth and African American, Native American, and Hispanic youth)?

▶ Have students work in groups of four to complete the "Educational Equality" handout on page 48. Facilitate a classroom discussion concerning their findings.

ACTIVITY THREE:

▶ Have students analyze "Woodson Quotes" (pg. 61) and write an essay explaining their relevance today.

ACTIVITY FOUR:

▶ Have students research the origin of the N-word and analyze the use of the term today.
INSTRUCTIONAL STRATEGY: Have students research the origin and use of the "N" word and devise a plan to motivate people in society, especially their own generation, to eliminate it from their vocabulary. Emphasize in this assignment self-determination and the importance of young people taking control of their present and future.

ACTIVITY FIVE:

▶ Have students choose a significant event they learned from this lesson to plot on their timeline.

Lesson FOUR

HANDOUTS AND MATERIALS

WOODSON QUOTES

Lesson Four: Education and Reform

"As another has well said, to handicap a student by teaching him that his black face is a curse and that his struggle to change his condition is hopeless is the worst sort of lynching. It kills one's aspirations and dooms him to vagabondage and crime. It is strange, then, that the friends of truth and the promoters of freedom have not risen up against the present propaganda in the schools and crushed it. This crusade is much more important than the anti-lynching movement, because there would be no lynching if it did not start in the schoolroom. Why not exploit, enslave, or exterminate a class that everybody is taught to regard as inferior" (Mis-Education, p. 4)

"Let the light of history enable us to see that "enough of good there is in the lowest estate to sweeten life; enough of evil in the highest to check presumption; enough there is of both in all estates to bind us in compassionate brotherhood, to teach us impressively that we are of one dying and one immortal family." Let truth destroy the dividing prejudices of nationality and teach universal love without distinction of race, merit or rank. With the sublime enthusiasm and heavenly vision of the Great Teacher let us help men to rise above the race hate of this age unto the altruism of a rejuvenated universe" (Observances, p. 24).

Woodson, C.G. (2002). Observances of Negro History Week. *Black History Bulletin*, 65, 1-35.

LET'S LOOK AT EDUCATIONAL EQUITY!

Complete the following activities to learn more about your school and educational community.

Find out!

What is the status of educational equity in your community? What is the per pupil spending rate for the schools in your district? How many ninth graders enter your school in a given year? How many of those ninth graders graduate from high school four years later?

What are the college-attendance rates for students who attend your high school? How many of the students who graduate in your district are eligible to attend college?

Find out!

The Fourteenth Amendment to the U.S. Constitution guarantees all citizens "equal protection under the law." In the BROWN decision, the Supreme Court ruled that Southern states had violated this principle for almost 70 years by forcing African Americans and others into separate schools and facilities. Whose job is it to make sure the government follows its own laws? What are some ways that communities can hold their government accountable? What might be the risks of speaking out against government policies and practices? Find examples. What might be the benefits of speaking out? Find examples.

How can you help your peers understand the importance of education? Remember, your best witness is not what you say, but what you do.

Slave vs. Enslaved Scenarios

Review the definition of "Modern-Day UGRR" concept (Key Terms pg. 80). With this concept in mind, read the scenarios below and decide whether the person is a slave or enslaved.

Scenario One: J. Doe grows up in a very sheltered environment and has not been exposed to people of different cultures. In fact, this young person's parents have taught against people of other cultures, and the family practices racism. J. Doe grows up only knowing people of his/her own culture. At age 18, J. Doe goes off to college, and the roommate is of another culture. The roommate turns out to be an exceptionally friendly person, and although J. Doe cannot find the courage to respond to the kindness, the roommate responds with kindness anyway. A whole school year passes, and J. Doe still treats the roommate with disrespect. Is J. Doe a slave or enslaved?

Scenario Two: You were recently hired at a very prestigious company. It is your first job and you are very excited about the possibilities for promotion. Your supervisor is a very well-known and authoritative figure in the company. In fact, your supervisor is the president of the company. This supervisor asks you to conduct some business for the company that you know is illegal. You refuse to do it, and the supervisor fires you under other pretenses. Are you a slave or enslaved?

Scenario Three: Joe and Jerry visit their uncle's home for his 50th birthday party. Their uncle runs out of ice and asks Joe and Jerry to take his car to the corner store for ice. They get into the car and immediately drive away because the need to return with the ice is urgent (Just think, a party with no ice.). A taillight is out on the car, and the police stop them. The police decide to search the car and find marijuana in the glove compartment. Joe and Jerry are taken to the police precinct and arrested. Are Joe and Jerry slaves or enslaved?

Scenario Four: A fourteen-year-old girl visits her fifteen-year-old cousin for spring break. The cousin plans to attend a party with her nineteen-year-old boyfriend who she knows is not accepted by her guardian, but she lies and says she is going to dinner at Red Lobster with friends. The girl visiting knows the whole plan and feels very uncomfortable about the lie, but without even discouraging her cousin, she leaves with the cousin anyway. The party ends up having several older boys present drinking alcohol and drugs. The cousin gets drunk, and the girl feels she should call her aunt but, again, decides not to do so. Eventually, the party gets out of hand. One of the older boys approaches the girl for sex. She refuses him and is raped. Is the girl a slave or enslaved?

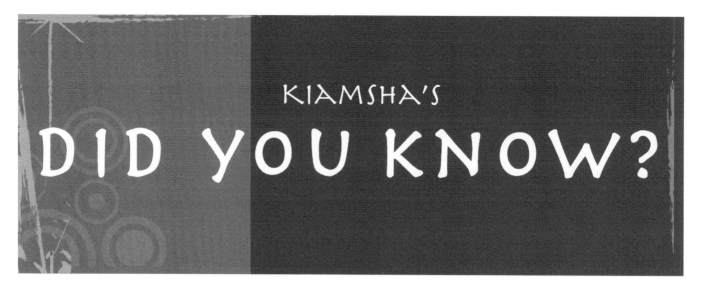

KIAMSHA'S
DID YOU KNOW?

The Persistence of Educational Inequity

DID YOU KNOW that school segregation is not a thing of the past? Today, schools in the North, South, East, and West are significantly segregated. Check out the following facts from the state of California.

▶ DID YOU KNOW that in May 2000, a coalition of civil rights groups filed the suit Williams v. California on the anniversary of the Brown v. Board of Education decision? The Williams case charged that the state of California had failed to live up to its constitutional obligation to provide "basic educational equity"[1]

▶ DID YOU KNOW that 37% of California's African American students attend "intensely segregated minority" schools?[2]

▶ DID YOU KNOW that these intensely segregated minority schools are more likely than majority White schools to experience shortages of college preparatory courses and adequately trained teachers for these courses?

▶ DID YOU KNOW that these intensely segregated minority schools have a 50% graduation rate for African American and Latino students?[3] (This means that only half of the entering ninth graders graduate four years later!) (California Educational Opportunity Report: Roadblocks to College, 2006)

▶ DID YOU KNOW that these intensely segregated minority schools spend less money per pupil to educate their students?[4]

  ▪ Schools with 90-100% students of color are located in school districts that spend an average of $6634 per student (per year)
  ▪ Schools with 50-89% students of color are located in districts that spend an average of $6837 per student
  ▪ Schools with 0-4% students of color are located in school districts that spend an average of $7,268 per student.

▶ DID YOU KNOW that performance in mathematics helps determine proficiency for many colleges and universities? A recent study of two significantly segregated middle schools found that only 6% of the schools' African American sixth-graders scored at or above grade proficiency in mathematics.[5]

KIAMSHA CONCEPT:
SLAVE vs ENSLAVED

SLAVE: Someone who willingly gives up their freedom to someone or something

ENSLAVED: To have one's freedom taken against her or his will

KEY TERMS

Scientific research – The means by which researchers are able to make conclusive statements about their studies with a minimum of bias.

Mob-sanctioned Murder – The practice of murder by extrajudicial (outside the normal course of legal proceedings) mob action. The accused is usually assumed guilty by large groups of people convinced of the person's guilt. Lynching was the most popular mob activity, and rarely were lynchers punished, or even arrested, for their crimes.

Anti-lynching – Resistance against lynch mob violence and government complicity in that violence. Lynchings occurred in the United States chiefly from the late 1700s through the 1960s.

Atrocity – Extremely evil or cruel condition, quality, or behavior.

Indelible – Incapable of being removed; permanent; making a mark not easily erased or washed away

Hierarchy – A group of persons organized or classified according to authority or rank

Religious Belief – Reverence for a supernatural power accepted as the creator or governor of the universe; the spiritual or emotional attitude of one who recognizes the existence of a superhuman power or powers

Implicit – Implied or understood, although not directly expressed; without doubts or reservations; contained in the nature of someone or something, although not readily apparent.

Impetus – A driving force; something that incites

Derive – To arrive at by reasoning; deduce or infer; to trace the origin or development of; to produce or obtain from another substance by chemical reaction

Presumption – The act of accepting as true; acceptance or belief based on reasonable evidence

Compassionate – Sympathetic; to have or display sympathy for another or for a situation

Sublime – Noble; majestic; of high spiritual, moral, or intellectual worth; not to be excelled; supreme; inspiring awe

Altruism – Selfless regard or concern for the well being of others

Rejuvenate – To restore youthful appearance or vigor; to stimulate to renewed activity; to uplift

Insightful – Having or showing the capacity to discern the true nature of a situation; instinctive

Distinction – The condition of being dissimilar; difference; a special feature or quality conferring superiority; honor

Exploit – To make use of unethically or selfishly; to utilize to the greatest advantage

Exterminate – To drive out; to destroy completely

Propaganda – Information spread abroad reflecting distinctive views, interests, opinions, doctrine, or allegations

Crusade – A vigorous, concerted movement against an abuse or for a cause

Aspiration – Strong desire for high achievement; an object of such desire; ambition; goal

Marxist – A believer in or follower of the ideas of Karl Marx and Friedrich Engels; a militant Communist

1) *HOW* DOES THE SLAVE VS ENSLAVED CONCEPT PROVIDE A NEW PERSPECTIVE WHEN CONNECTING HISTORY TO PRESENT EVENTS?

2) *NAME* THE PRECURSOR OF THE NAACP AND THE PERIOD OF TIME IT OPERATED IN THE UNITED STATES.

3) *ANALYZE* AND DISCUSS RE-SEGREGATION TODAY IN LIGHT OF HISTORICAL EVENTS. **FOR EXAMPLE**: RE-SEGREGATION HAS CAUSED CLASSROOMS ACROSS THE UNITED STATES OF AMERICA TO BECOME DOMINATED BY ONE CULTURAL/ETHNIC GROUP RATHER THAN MULTI-CULTURAL.

Lesson FIVE

Charting the Past

GOAL:

Students will research each decade from 1840 to present and record at least three significant events or prominent people in that timeframe. Students will examine especially the horror of mob-sanctioned murder orchestrated through lynching. Students may use the discoveries noted on the accompanying DVD as a reference.

ACTIVITY ONE:

▶ Distribute and review with students "Kiamsha Concept: How to Break a Bad Habit" (pg. 79).

   INSTRUCTIONAL STRATEGY: Have students complete the "Breaking Bad Habits" exercise on page 76. Have students share their answers with the class.

▶ Distribute and review with students "Key Terms" (pg. 80).

▶ Review with students "Kiamsha's Did You Know?" trivia (pg. 78).

ACTIVITY TWO:

▶ Have students view "Chapter Five" on the DVD. As they view the film, have students record all historical facts discussed in the students' dialogue on the DVD.

▶ Have students choose a significant event they learned from this DVD segment to plot on their ongoing timeline.

▶ Have students draft a letter in response to Dr. Cosby's views shared at the Brown v. Board of Education Anniversary Celebration that are noted on the film.

▶ Distribute "Woodson Quotes" (pg. 75) and have students write an essay that analyzes the quote in relation to the mentality of individuals who participated in and condoned lynch mobs and also the mentality of youth who participate in and condone negative peer pressure.

ACTIVITY THREE:

▶ Organize a community viewing of the documentary *Freedom's Song: 100 Years of African American Struggle and Triumph* (2007), and show the following three segments: "The Niagara Movement," "Tulsa Race Riots," and "The Poor People's Campaign." Aim to attract a multicultural audience, and after the viewing, facilitate a discussion about events highlighted in the segments. Encourage audience members to organize a viewing of the entire DVD in their own communities and families. Also, organize an essay contest among students and have them write about the significance of the events highlighted in the film and how knowledge of history can change race relations in the United States.

   OPTIONAL: Ask your school, church, or neighborhood choir to form a multicultural choir and perform with full choreography Kiamsha's version of "Lift Ev'ry Voice and Sing." (Visit the Curriculum Guide Resources link at www.kiamshayouth.org to view performance of the song)

ACTIVITY FOUR:

▶ Distribute "Significant Events in History" handout (pg. 77), and organize students into groups of four. Have groups prepare a timeline that charts segregation in the U.S. and also charts the resegregation of public schools in the 21st century. They may use the handout as a reference or starting point for research. Have teams share their findings with the class.

ACTIVITY FIVE:

▶ Quiz students with "How Much Do You Remember" trivia (pg. 81).

Lesson FIVE

HANDOUTS AND MATERIALS

WOODSON QUOTES

Lesson Five: Charting the Past

"On the other hand, just as thorough education in the belief in the equality of races has brought the world to the cat-and-dog stage of religious and racial strife, so may thorough instruction in the equality of races bring about a reign of brotherhood through an appreciation of the virtues of all races, creeds, and colors. In such a millennium the achievements of the Negro properly set forth will crown him as a factor in early human progress and a maker of modern civilization. He has supplied the demand for labor of a large area of our country, he has been a conservative force in its recent economic development; he has given the nation a poetic stimulus; he has developed the most popular music of the modern era; and he has preserved in its purity the brotherhood taught by Jesus of Nazareth. In his native country, moreover, he produced in the ancient world a civilization contemporaneous with that of the nations of the early Mediterranean, he influenced the cultures then cast in the crucible of time, and he taught the modern world the use of iron by which science and initiative have remade the universe. Must we let this generation continue ignorant of these eloquent facts?" (p. 23)

Woodson, C.G. (2002). Observances of Negro History Week. *Black History Bulletin*, 65, 1-35.

On the back of this paper, make a list of good habits that are repeated daily.

Review the examples below of bad habits. List what could be put off and put on to break these bad habits.

Example:	Put Off	Put On
Stealing	stealing	hard work; giving to others

1) Nail biting   _____   _____

2) Lying   _____   _____

3) Use of Illegal Drugs   _____   _____

4) Sexting   _____   _____

5) Shoplifting   _____   _____

6) Cheating on Exams   _____   _____

7) Plagiarism   _____   _____

SLAVERY TIMELINE	**(1619 -1865)**
CONSTITUTION OF THE UNITED STATES OF AMERICA	**(1787)**
FUGITIVE SLAVE ACT	**(1850)**
DRED SCOTT DECISION	**(1857)**
CIVIL WAR	**(1861)**
PRESIDENT LINCOLN SIGNS EMANCIPATION PROCLAMATION	**(1863)**
PRESIDENT LINCOLN RECOMMENDS DEPORTATION OF THE NEGRO	**(1862)**
RECONSTRUCTION	**(1865 – 1877)**
BEGINNING OF FORMAL PUBLIC EDUCATION OF THE NEGRO	**(1865)**
BLACK CODES	**(1865)**
KU KLUX KLAN	**(1866)**
PLESSY V. FERGUSON	**(1896)**
JAMES WELDON JOHNSON WRITES POEM "LIFT EVERY VOICE AND SING"	**(1900)**
PUBLICATION OF *THE SOULS OF BLACK FOLK*	**(1903)**
NIAGARA MOVEMENT	**(1905)**
NAACP	**(1909)**
NATIONAL URBAN LEAGUE	**(1910)**
WORLD WAR I	**(1914 – 1918)**
BIRTH OF A NATION RELEASED	**(1915)**
ASSOCIATION FOR THE STUDY OF AFRICAN AMERICAN LIFE AND HISTORY	**(1915)**
SEPARATION OF THE EDUCATED NEGRO FROM HIS LESS FORTUNATE BROTHER	**(1930s)**
PUBLICATION OF *THE MIS-EDUCATION OF THE NEGRO*	**(1933)**
WORLD WAR II	**(1939 – 1945)**
PEARL HARBOUR	**(1941)**
CIVIL RIGHTS MOVEMENT	**(1955 – 1965)**
BROWN V. BOARD OF EDUCATION	**(1954)**
BROWN II – "ALL DELIBERATE SPEED"	**(1955)**
THE CLINTON TWELVE	**(1956)**
THE LITTLEROCK NINE	**(1957)**
REMOTE CONTROL – INTERNET EVOLUTION	**(1957 – PRESENT)**
STUDENT NON-VIOLENT COORDINATING COMMITTEE (SNCC)	**(1960)**
THE CHILDRENS' MARCH IN BIRMINGHAM, ALABAMA	**(1963)**
CIVIL RIGHTS ACT (1964) AND VOTING RIGHTS ACT	**(1965)**
CONGRESS DID NOT PASS ANY OF THE ANTI-LYNCHING LAWS INTRODUCED	**(1977)**
MILLION MAN MARCH	**(1995)**
KIAMSHA (IN PARTNERSHIP WITH INTFA) WINS YWCA US/CANADA "STOP RACISM YOUTH CHALLENGE	**(2000)**
KIAMSHA RELEASES ORIGINAL RENDITION, "LIFT EVERY VOICE AND SING"	**(2000)**
FIRST APOLOGY BY CONGRESS FOR NOT DOING MORE TO STOP THE ATROCITIES OF THE 1860s	**(2005)**
"GIRL LIKE ME" RELEASEDE RE-ENACTMENT OF 1954 DOLL EXPERIMENT	**(2006)**
PEN OR PENCIL YOUTH-LED MOVEMENT TO END VIOLENCE, HIGH SCHOOL DROPOUTS, AND ENTERING PRISON	**(2007)**
CONGRESS PASSES RESOLUTION APOLOGIZING FOR SLAVERY	**(2008)**
ASALH RELEASES *CARTER G. WOODSON'S APPEAL* WRITTEN IN 1921	**(2008)**
FIRST AFRICAN AMERICAN PRESIDENT OF THE UNITED STATES OF AMERICA ELECTED	**(2008)**
ASALH'S FIRST SERIES OF "WOODSON TALKS"–COURAGEOUS CONVERSATIONS ON RACE	**(2009)**
SILENT EPIDEMIC AND HIGH COST RESEARCH RELEASED	**(2009)**
PEN OR PENCIL STUDENT NO VIOLENCE COORDINATING CORPORATIONS (SNCC) FORMED	**(2009)**
DASHOLOGY (*THE SCIENCE OF SERVICE*) IS INTRODUCED TO PUBLIC AT CONGRESSIONAL BLACK CAUCUS	**(2009)**
YOUTH-LED MARCH ON WASHINGTON FOR MENTORS AND AGAINST VIOLENCE	**(2010)**
INTERNATIONAL YEAR FOR PEOPLE OF AFRICAN DESCENT BY UNITED NATIONS	**(2011)**

DID YOU KNOW?

Did you know that the 1963 Children's March in Birmingham, AL was in part the reason for the bombing at 16th Street Baptist Church in Birmingham, AL that killed four innocent, little girls?

Did you know the names of these girls are Addie Mae Collins, Denise McNair, Carole Robinson, and Cynthia Wesley? Begin today speaking their names.

KIAMSHA CONCEPT:
How to Break a Bad Habit

Breaking a bad habit is a put on/put off process

A thief does not stop being a thief simply because he stops stealing—the thief must put off stealing and put on something equally as desirous to replace the desire to steal. For example, the thief could put on hard work and giving to others in need

Seared Conscience

When you ignore your conscience screaming at you with the right thing to do for so long that you no longer hear the right information—doing wrong becomes a way of life, with no remorse. At this point, your conscience has become seared

Modern-Day Underground Railroad Concept – Reveals the fact that during the era of enslavement, there were no slaves but people who were enslaved by their slave masters. However, youth and adults today have become slaves to the modern-day slave masters known as alcohol and other drugs, premarital sexual activity, violence, racial disharmony, jealousy, envy, and the list goes on. Kiamsha challenges you to use the same level of conviction the enslaved people used in the era of enslavement—they did whatever it took to free themselves from the slave master. They even walked miles in unhealthy and tiring conditions—whatever it took.

Absolute Truth – That which is true for all people, for all times, for all places. Absolute truth is objective (defined outside of ourselves), universal (for all people), and constant (for all times)

Slave – Someone who willingly gives up their freedom to someone or something

Enslaved – To have one's freedom taken against her or his will

Seared Conscience – Your conscience is a gift. It is your inner sense of right and wrong. A seared or withered conscience develops when you continue to ignore its promptings, urgings, and screams telling you to do the right thing. Eventually, you don't hear it anymore. At this point, it is seared

Self-Determination - The right of a people to choose their own destiny

Culture – The totality of socially transmitted behavior patterns, arts, beliefs, institutions, and all other products of human work and thought typical of a population or community at a given time
Example: Teenagers are a culture. Teachers are a culture.

Conviction – A basic moral principle that you purpose to follow no matter what the costs. Convictions never change

Preference – A decision that changes from situation to situation

Compromising Situation – a condition that someone places themselves in that makes it difficult for them to uphold their convictions

Innate – Possessed at birth
Example: Everyone was born with the innate ability to know right from wrong

Character – The combination of emotional, intellectual, and moral qualities distinguishing one person from another; distinctive feature or attribute; moral or ethical strength; INTEGRITY

Qualities of Life – Character traits that can only be developed with the help of the Spirit within you. The Spirit produces these character traits and we cannot obtain them by trying to get them by ourselves. Growth is gradual; man can assist producing it but cannot initiate it or assure its production. By obtaining all of these character traits, we can fulfill the intended purpose God has made us individually to fulfill. They are *love, joy, peace, longsuffering, gentleness, goodness (kindness), faithfulness, and self-control*

Integrity – Doing the right thing even when no one is looking

1) *WHAT* EVENT IN HISTORY IS THE PRECURSOR TO THE NATIONAL ASSOCIATION FOR THE ADVANCEMENT OF COLORED PEOPLE (NAACP)?

2) *BREAKING* A BAD HABIT IS A TWO-SIDED ENTERPRISE. IN OTHER WORDS, IT IS A ___ ___ AND ___ ___ PROCESS. (FILL IN THE BLANKS)

3) *COMPARE* THE MINDSET OF LYNCH MOBS IN THE EARLY 1900S TO THE MINDSET OF THOSE TODAY WHO ENGAGE IN NEGATIVE PEER PRESSURE. WRITE OR DISCUSS A BRIEF SUMMARY OF THEIR SIMILARITIES.

Lesson SIX

The Future: As the Youth See It

Lesson SIX

GOAL:

Students will prepare for the future by creating a plan to leave the world in a better place than it is today. Achieving this future goal will require students, first, to take personal responsibility to be individual leaders of integrity and, second, to work collectively, as families, organizations, schools, etc., to pursue everything in excellence so our world will be a better place to live.

ACTIVITY ONE:

▶ Have students view "Chapter Six" on the DVD.

▶ Distribute "Woodson Quotes" handout (pg. 89).

INSTRUCTIONAL STRATEGY: Have students work in groups of four to research and gather news articles that highlight "enlightened" youth who have taken their destiny into their own hands. Have groups share their findings with the class.

ACTIVITY TWO:

▶ Distribute and review with students "Key Terms" (pg. 94).

INSTRUCTIONAL STRATEGY: Have students complete the "Qualities of Life" handout on page 91 and share their answers with the class.

▶ Distribute the handout "And So I Choose" (pg. 93) and have students meditate on the poem and its meaning each day for two weeks. Inform them that this time could be as little as ten to thirty minutes or as long as one or two hours—whatever works for them. They should aim to remove distractions during this time, television, phones, other people, or the computer, for example, and reflect. During the two-week period, students should study the definitions of all of the qualities of life and utilize them in their interaction with others on a daily basis. Inform them that embodying these qualities will be the beginning of their contribution to making the world a better place to live.

▶ Have students keep a daily journal of their thoughts and events of the day during this two-week period, and at the end of two weeks, have students report on their daily perspective and life events for the past two weeks.

ACTIVITY THREE:

▶ Have students read the letter the Kiamsha Youth Empowerment Organization wrote to Dr. John Hope Franklin, noted historian and mentee of Dr. Carter G. Woodson (Father of Black History), for Dr. Franklin's 94th birthday in January 2009 (pgs. 98-99).

▶ Have students read the letter written by the Powell House Project (PHP) participants (youth who are being mentored by Kiamsha) (pg. 100). Have students compare and discuss the ideas Kiamsha and the Powell House Project youth have for "How to Make the World a Better Place to Live."

INSTRUCTIONAL STRATEGY: With the Franklin and Powell House letters in mind, have students create a class list of "How to Make the World a Better Place to Live," being careful not to duplicate items on previous lists.

▶ Have class brainstorm a creative way to publicize their list, and have them share the list with their school community. Have class brainstorm way(s) to get other youth involved in thinking about and following through with actions that can make the world a better place to live. Have students share the challenge and the lists (Kiamsha, PHP, and class list) with others in their community in order to encourage them to think positively and to make better decisions.

ACTIVITY Four:

▶ Have students revisit the key term "self-determination" and brainstorm ways their generation can begin to take charge of their own destiny. Have students discuss how the world might be different if they influenced their peers to stop and think about everything they did before they did it and used the key terms, concepts, and their knowledge of history to make better decisions. Have students discuss how the world might change if lots of people changed their negative ways of thinking.

▶ Challenge students to share with their peers the Kiamsha concepts, key terms, and historical facts they have learned in this unit, and challenge them to encourage their peers to "Stop and Think."

▶ Review with students the Kiamsha Concept "S.T.A.R.," and have students work in groups of four to complete the "Stop and Think" handout (pg. 95).

▶ Have each student complete the "What If?" exercise (pg. 96) and share his or her answers with the class. Emphasize for students the significance of using the S.T.A.R. (Stop, Think, Act and Review) method to combat many of the ills that exists in our society. Explain to students that knowledge of history will help improve racial harmony in this country. Challenge them to find opportunities to encourage the study of history in their school. Also, challenge students to encourage positive behavior among their peers such as academic achievement, abstinence from premarital sex, alcohol and other drugs, violence, and prejudice.

INSTRUCTIONAL STRATEGY: Have students create posters that depict their "What If?" ideas and how things would be different if everyone stopped and thought before they acted or made decisions.

ACTIVITY Five:

▶ Distribute the "Family Mission Statement" handout (pg. 90) and have students organize their families to create a family mission statement.

▶ Have students conduct an interview with a family member, neighbor, or family friend who lived during segregation and experienced integration as a child in school.

INSTRUCTIONAL STRATEGY: Have students write a report of the interview they conducted. Gather students' reports and create a newspaper that shares the stories of all the people interviewed.

ACTIVITY Six:

▶ Use the following question to stimulate discussion, "Do you believe someone can have something in their heart that they did not know was there that may cause them to lash out in anger?"

▶ Distribute the "Anger" handout (pg. 97) and discuss with students the affects of this emotion. Emphasize to students that "anger is a secondary emotion" and that they must identify the primary emotion that caused their anger. Explain to students that although there may be historical events that anger them, they should look at history objectively.

ACTIVITY Seven:

▶ Have the class reconnect with virtual pen pals/students from Africa, and have students share with them their plans for "How to Make the World a Better Place to Live" and the song "Rainbow of Love" from the *Pathways* cd.

Lesson SIX

HANDOUTS AND MATERIALS

WOODSON QUOTES

Lesson Six: The Future—As the Youth See It

"The world does not want and will never have the heroes and heroines of the past. What this age needs is an enlightened youth not to undertake the tasks like theirs, but to imbibe the spirit of the great men and answer the present call to duty with equal nobleness of soul " (Mis-Education, p. 77)

FAMILY MISSION STATEMENT – WHAT IS IT?

Create a mission statement for your family using the following questions as a guide.

What is the purpose of our family?
What kind of family do we want to be?
What kinds of things do we want to do?
What kind of feeling do we want to have in our home?
What kind of relationships do we want to have with one another?
What things are truly important to us as a family?
What are our family's highest priorities/goals?
What are the unique talents, gifts, and abilities of family members?
What are our responsibilities as family members?
What are the principles and guidelines we want our family to follow?
Who are our heroes? What is it about them that we like and would like to emulate?
What family members inspire us, and why do they inspire us?
What families inspire us, and why do we admire them?
How can we contribute to society as a family and become more service-oriented?
ADD YOUR OWN STATEMENT(S) / COMMON VISION(S)

MISSION STATEMENT SAMPLE ONE

Value honesty with others and ourselves
Create an environment where each of us can find support and encouragement in achieving our life's goals
Respect and accept each person's unique personality and talents
Promote a loving, kind, and happy atmosphere
Support family endeavors that better society
Maintain patience through understanding
Always resolve conflicts with each other rather than harboring anger
Promote the realization of life's treasures

MISSION STATEMENT SAMPLE TWO

To love each other
To help each other
To believe in each other
To wisely use our time, talents, and resources to bless others
To worship together forever

MISSION STATEMENT SAMPLE THREE

Our family will be a place where we, along with our friends and guests, find joy, comfort, peace, and happiness. We will seek to create a clean and orderly environment that is livable and comfortable. We will exercise wisdom in what we choose to eat, read, see, and do at home. We want to teach our children to love, learn, laugh, and work and develop their unique talents.

Identify the qualities of life you must exhibit in each case below in order to come through the situation using the power of your Spirit within you.

1. Getting fired from a job

2. Your team experiences a championship defeat

3. You were cooking a meal for mom and began watching a favorite show. Your pot roast burned to a crisp

4. The dog messed on a freshly shampooed carpet

5. A loved one dies

6. Wake up late for school and can't find the notebook that you placed all your homework in

7. Rushing to school and blouse/shirt needs ironing. The bus will be here in 5 minutes and as you iron the blouse/shirt, the iron is too hot and you scorch the item right in front. All other tops you would wear with that pair of pants are dirty

8. Your parents have allowed a cousin to live with you. The girl is a brat and is constantly getting into your belongings without permission. You know your parents have talked to the child many times, but the action continues. Your mom informs you that the child is very depressed and urges you to be patient while they seek help for the child. You treat the cousin with love even though it bothers you a great deal when someone invades your privacy

9. You have an illness that causes you a lot of pain. You have prayed to God to ease the pain but it appears God is taking forever to do so

10. A family has a fire in their home, and you supply them with clothes, even a place to stay until they can get on their feet

11. A friend at school has had a bad morning fighting with parents and cannot seem to stop crying after getting off the bus at school. You offer them a tissue, and with a warm smile, you let them know you're there if they need you

12. A group of your friends decide to skip school. There are nine of you, and you decide not to follow. They tease you, call you names, and try to coerce you to follow, but you stand fast to your decision.

13. A male or female friend tries to entice you to come over when his or her parents are not present. You know exactly what is on your friend's mind because it is on your mind, as well. You decide it's better not to go, no matter how inviting it sounds.

14. You and a friend have a fight two hours earlier. Your friend calls you distraught because he or she has experienced a real, heart-felt hurt in an ongoing relationship. You put aside the disagreement for the moment to soothe your friend's pain.

ANSWER KEY

Identify the qualities of life you must exhibit in each case below in order to come through the situation using the power of your Spirit within you.

1. Getting fired from a job. (Joy)

2. Your team experiences a championship defeat. (Joy)

3. Cooking a meal for mom and began watching a favorite show—Pot roast burned to a crisp. (Peace)

4. The dog messed on a freshly shampooed carpet. (Peace)

5. A loved one dies. (Joy, Peace)

6. Wake up late for school and can't find the notebook that you placed all your homework in. (Patience, Joy, Peace, Self Control)

7. Rushing to school and blouse/shirt needs ironing. The bus will be here in 5 minutes and as you iron the blouse/shirt, the iron is too hot and you scorch the item right in front. All other tops you would wear with that pair of pants are dirty. (Patience, Peace)

8. Your parents have allowed a cousin to live with you. The girl is a brat and is constantly getting into your belongings without permission. You know your parents have talked to the child many times, but the action continues. Your mom informs you that the child is very depressed and urges you to be patient while they seek help for the child. You treat the cousin with love even though it bothers you a great deal when someone invades your privacy. (Longsuffering)

9. You have an illness that causes you a lot of pain. You have prayed to God to ease the pain, but it appears God is taking forever to do so. (longsuffering)

10. A family has a fire in their home – you supply them with clothes, even a place to stay until they can get on their feet. (gentleness/kindness)

11. A friend at school has had a bad morning fighting with parents and cannot seem to stop crying after getting off the bus at school. You offer them a tissue, and with a warm smile, you let them know you're there if they need you. (gentleness/kindness)

12. A group of your friends decide to skip school. There are nine of you, and you decide not to follow. They tease you, call you names, and try to coerce you to follow, but you stand fast to your decision. (self-control)

13. A male or female friend tries to entice you to come over when his or her parents are not present. You know exactly what is on his/her mind because it is on your mind as well. You decide it's better not to go, no matter how inviting it sounds. (self-control)

14. You and a friend have a fight two hours earlier. Your friend calls you distraught because he or she has experienced a real heart felt hurt in an ongoing relationship. You put aside the disagreement for the moment to soothe your friend's pain. (faithfulness)

AND SO I CHOOSE:

I choose love...

No occasion justifies hatred; no injustice warrants bitterness, I choose love.
Today I will love my Creator and what He loves.

I choose joy...

I will invite my Creator to be my source of circumstance. I will refuse the temptation to be cynical...the tool of the lazy thinker. I will refuse to see people as anything less than human beings, made by the Creator. I will refuse to see any problem as anything less than an opportunity to see my Creator and His creation.

I choose peace...

I will overlook the inconveniences of the world. Instead of cursing the one who takes my place, I'll invite him to do so. Rather than complaining that the wait is too long, I will thank my Creator for a moment to pray. Instead of clinching my fist at new assignments, I will face them with joy and courage.

I choose kindness...

I will be kind to the poor, for they are alone. Kind to the rich, for they are afraid. And kind to the unkind, for such is how my Creator has treated me.

I choose goodness...

I will go without a dollar before I take a dishonest one. I will be overlooked before I will boast. I will confess before I will accuse. I choose goodness.

I choose faithfulness...

Today I will keep my promises. My debtors and my friends will not regret their trust in me.
My associates will not question my word. My wife will not question my love. And my children will never fear that their father will not come home.

I choose gentleness...

Nothing is won by force. I choose to be gentle. If I raise my voice may it be only in praise. If I clench my fist, may it be only in prayer. If I make a demand, may it be only of myself.

I choose self-control...

I am a spiritual being. After this body is dead, my spirit will soar.
My soul will be destined to where I send it.
I refuse to let what will rot (my body of flesh) and is temporal, rule the eternal (my soul). I choose self-control.

I will be drunk only by joy. I will be impassioned only by my faith. I will be influenced only by my Creator. I will be taught only by my spirit within which my Source has given me. I choose self-control.

Love, joy, peace, patience, kindness, goodness, faithfulness, gentleness, and self-control. To these I commit my day. If I succeed, I will give thanks to my Creator who is my source for all things. If I fail, I will seek His grace. And then when this day is done I will place my head on my pillow and rest for a night or eternity—because tomorrow is not promised.

Author Unknown

LOVE — To have and to show compassion toward others; love is an action word; love is unconditional—it does not require anything from the person being loved

MEEKNESS – Power under control; meekness is not weakness

PEACE – A joyous sense of well-being that views all things as good; incomprehensible contentment in the midst of trials and tribulations

GENTLENESS/KINDNESS – Being forgiving and generous; our kindness must not be selective; someone who is kind is predisposed to do good unto others

LONGSUFFERING – Sitting still and waiting until the Creator moves in your situation; the ability to keep going when you want to quit

FAITHFULNESS – The quality of reliability, trustworthiness, dependability, and loyalty. We learn to be faithful by our Creator's faithfulness to us

JOY – The presence of the Creator within—expressing his character outwardly—even in times of great difficulty and disappointment. Our joy is closely aligned with our faith

GOODNESS – The desire to give a person all that is helpful and beneficial to them

PATIENCE – Peacefully enduring people or situations that challenge you; keeping a calm temperament

SELF-CONTROL – Restraining one's desire; discipline; the practice of thinking things through before you act

MAKE THE WORLD A BETTER PLACE TO LIVE!

STOP AND THINK

THE SCENARIO

It's a Saturday night, and four friends are hanging out in one of their basements. One friend turns to the others and says, "I feel like killing somebody." Later, they all leave the house. As they are walking down the street, they see a couple standing at their car. The same friend repeats, "I feel like killing somebody." With his friends watching, he approaches the couple and carries out the murder. Soon after, all four friends are caught, charged, and convicted of the crime.

WHAT IF at least one of the people involved would have stopped to think?

Using the principles we have discussed recently, write your own **WHAT IF** to show ways the situation above would have changed if at least one person's, out of the four, thought process had been guided by information that would invoke different ways of thinking.

PRINCIPLES AND CONCEPTS

1. ABSOLUTE TRUTH
2. CONVICTION
3. I AM MY BROTHER'S KEEPER
4. DO AS I SAY, NOT AS I DO
5. QUALITIES OF LIFE
6. POINT OF CHOICE
7. INNATE ABILITY

CONSIDER THE FOLLOWING:

1. The ages of the four people in the scenario above ranged from 15 to 25. **WHAT IF** the oldest person had been thinking about the concept, "I am my brother's keeper"? How would the situation have changed?

2. **WHAT IF**, before leaving home, the oldest would have said to the youngest, "You are too young to hang with us. We'll check you later."

3. **WHAT IF** at least one person in the group had tried to reason with the person who said, "I feel like killing someone?" How could that have possibly changed what happened?

4. **WHAT IF** when the one who said he felt like killing someone, just one of the four had said, "Man, I'm out. You're on your own," and actually left the scene?

95

COME UP WITH AT LEAST FIVE
"WHAT IF'S"

1. *WHAT IF...*

2. *WHAT IF...*

3. *WHAT IF...*

4. *WHAT IF...*

5. *WHAT IF...*

JUST THINK: We are every part of this nation. If you STOPPED and THOUGHT about everything you did, before you did it, and allowed some of the qualities of life to guide your decisions, you may find your life to be much more productive and a blessing to others, as well as yourself.

WHAT IF... YOU DECIDED, using SELF-DETERMINATION, you would join with your peers who are thinking the same way as you to influence the small area where you live, go to school, go to church, etc? What do you think could possibly happen in your community??

WHAT IF...

ANGER, *WHAT IS IT?*

TRY TO DEFINE FIRST BEFORE READING DEFINITIONS BELOW

PONDER THE FOLLOWING QUESTION AND INCIDENT: Can you have anger inside and not know it?

<u>Example</u>: *Michael Richards, best known as Kramer*

<u>His comments on stage when a heckler taunted him</u> (2008): Fifty years ago we'd have you upside down with a f_ _ _ _ _ fork up your a _ _," he says while on stage. "You can talk, you can talk, you're brave now motherf _ _ _ _ _. Throw his a _ _ out. He's a n _ _ _ _ _! He's a   n _ _ _ _ _! He's a n _ _ _ _ _!

<u>His apology</u>: "For me to be at a comedy club and flip out and say this crap..." said Richards.

KEY STATEMENT: "50 YEARS AGO." WHERE WERE WE IN HISTORY 50 YEARS AGO? That was 10 years before Martin Luther King, Jr.'s assassination! That was only four years after Brown vs. Board of Education passed in the Supreme Court—but we were still fighting for our civil rights.

Do you accept his apology?

STOP AND THINK: Out of the abundance of the heart the mouth speaks. Above is a good example to help each of us understand why it is important to test what is in our heart. WHERE DID IT COME FROM? WHAT IS HIS POINT OF REFERENCE? WHAT IS YOUR POINT OF REFERENCE?

ANGER – A feeling of great displeasure, hostility, indignation or exasperation

- □ **INDIGNATION** – To regard as unworthy
    ANGER AROUSED BY ONE THAT IS UNJUST, MEAN, OR UNWORTHY
- □ **EXASPERATION** – Angry; IRRITATED
- □ **HOSTILITY** – Antagonism; FEELING OF ENMITY
- □ **ANTAGONISM** – The condition of being an opposing or competing principle, force, or factor
- □ **ENMITY** – DEEP ROOTED MUTUAL HATRED
- □ **HATRED** – Intense animosity, or hostility
- □ **ANIMOSITY** – LONG-STANDING OR DEEP-SEATED HOSTILITY; ENMITY
- □ **DEEP-SEATED** – deeply entrenched; ingrained
- □ **ENTRENCHED** – TO FIX FIRMLY, SECURELY; TO PROVIDE WITH A TRENCH IN ORDER TO FORTIFY OR DEFEND, SUCH AS "ENTRENCHED IN THEIR HISTORY"

STATEMENT: ANGER IS A SECONDARY EMOTION.

YOU MUST IDENTIFY THE PRIMARY EMOTION THAT CAUSED YOUR ANGER. YOU MUST. . .

- Acknowledge the anger
- Identify the primary emotion
    - □ Is it hurt, frustration, or insecurity?
- Then, consider the primary emotion
- Once you discover it, then apply some of the qualities of life that best apply.

THE CHOICE IS YOURS.

KIAMSHA YOUTH EMPOWERMENT ORGANIZATION

9440 Pennsylvania Avenue, Suite 120
Upper Marlboro, MD 20772-3659
Tel. (301)336-4586; Fax Number (301)336-6052; www.kiamshayouth.org

"that which awakens me"

January 2, 2009

Dear Dr. John Hope Franklin,

Happy Birthday Dr. Franklin, from the Kiamsha family that you have influenced greatly.

We greatly value your thoughts and ideas conveyed in your book, <u>Mirror to America</u>, and in your lecture, "Toward a Second American Revolution," which you presented at the Sacramento State University Ethnic Studies Center. You said in that lecture,

> We need a new declaration, a declaration in favor of the rights of all men [. . .] We need a new commitment to a more perfect union, one in which some are not more equal than others. We need a new adherence to the principles of equality. We need a New American Revolution that will create a new ideology of comradeship in the great enterprise of building a society in which every man and woman can face tomorrow unencumbered by the burdens of the past or the prejudices of the present. This calls for a revolution in the heart and soul of every American. That is what the first American Revolution did not have [. . .] This is what the New American Revolution must have.

That is our goal, Dr. Franklin, through the method of developing the fruit of the spirit on a personal level and exhibiting unconditional love for our fellow brothers and sisters. Unencumbered by their inability to understand or except the truth, we will take the lead to pursue a more perfect union through a revolution of the heart because we are armed with the truth.

We will never forget your words of wisdom spoken to us at the 2007 ASALH convention in Charlotte, North Carolina when we asked you the question, "What advice would you give us to combat the problem of race in our society today?" What you said to us that day still rings loudly in our spirit. You so eloquently and simplistically said to us that day, "It will be so wonderful when we finally realize how insignificant race is." HOW PROFOUND!

Dr. Franklin, we have heard your heart and have set out to reach as many of our peers as we can with the message that learning our history is not an option. We have also joined with our mentors and elders and developed a plan of action with goals inspired by your words in "Mirror to America." We have initiated a goal of ASALH to begin what is being called "Woodson Talks" around the country. These courageous

98

KIAMSHA YOUTH EMPOWERMENT ORGANIZATION

9440 Pennsylvania Avenue, Suite 120
Upper Marlboro, MD 20772-3659
Tel. (301)336-4586; Fax Number (301)336-6052; www.kiamshayouth.org

"that which awakens me"

conversations on race will be guided by the thoughts and ideas of the Father of Black History in not only his seminal work, *The Mis-Education of the Negro* (1933), but also in the manuscript that was lost for over 80 years, *Carter G. Woodson's Appeal* (1921).

Thank you for dedicating your life to this work and sharing your knowledge with others. Thank you for being inspired by the legacy of Dr. Carter G. Woodson because through you, we imagine meeting Dr. Woodson face to face. We love you, and you can count on us to continue your legacy that so richly connects us to the life and work of Dr. Woodson.

As the Word of God says, "to whom much is given...much is required." We have been given much, and you are a large part of our multitude of blessings. You can trust us to take up the mantel as a chosen remnant of our generation to educate others, starting with our own generation, to ensure that we will not leave the problem of race for another unknowing, innocent generation to solve. We will then join our mentors in reaching the silent, baby boomers and X generations to help their peers understand the importance of mentoring someone to share their wisdom before they leave this earth. This is a year of transition, and we are thankful to be a part of this wonderful move of God.

We love you, Dr. Franklin! Thank you for the example you have left for so many to follow. Happy 94th Birthday!

Sincerely,

Kiamsha Youth Empowerment Organization and its entire village

HOW TO MAKE THE WORLD A BETTER PLACE TO LIVE....

50 YEARS FROM NOW

Narrative compiled by Sabria Hipps and Maria Hall, Powell House Project Youth Employees

The youth in America need to take a part in making this world a better place to live. As we witnessed in "The Children's March of 1963," the children took a lead in the changes that needed to be made in the Civil Rights Movement. Today we are suffering from some really bad situations—situations that, if we were taught differently, we would probably change some of our ways. What we have decided after receiving the training we have been exposed to in the Powell House Project, is that it is going to again have to be the youth who step up to the plate and help their peers change what is happening in our world. We need to contribute to making the world a better place to live because people are looking at us wondering what in the world has happened to the youth. Many of us are failing in school, killing each other, disrespecting adults, disrespecting our teachers, being disruptive in our classrooms, using drugs, and getting pregnant at very young ages, doing so much that should not be a part of our lives. Where did it start, and where and how will it end? It started with our lives being connected with some adults who were not positive. And when we do have positive adults, our peers who do not, help to influence their peers. We no longer want to make this an excuse, but we want to acknowledge this as the reason and use our innate ability to determine right from wrong. We have decided to look at some areas we can start to change now.

A list was started at a Kiamsha Youth Conference in 1996. They shared the list with us, and we have adopted their list and now added to the list. We will keep reaching out to our generation to help us add to the list and begin to live this in our daily lives. If we do, fifty years from now, the world will look differently for our children, and our children's children.
WE WILL STRIVE TO:

1996 KIAMSHA CONFERENCE PARTICIPANTS LIST

NEVER drive without a license
WEAR a seat belt because it is the law
NEVER allow my friends to charge me less for purchases illegally—the hook up [THIS IS STEALING]*
NEVER charge my friends less for purchases
NEVER walk on a red light [because it is the law] *
NEVER cheat on exams
NEVER use profanity
NEVER drink & smoke as a teen
NEVER use a fake ID
NEVER hold a grudge
NEVER steal
NEVER lie
NEVER allow jealousy to control me
NEVER gamble [NEGATIVE RISK-TAKING ONLY]**
NEVER disrespect adults . . . teachers in classrooms
NEVER cheat others in any situation
NEVER hook [SKIP] school*
NEVER fight

2009 POWELL HOUSE PROJECT YOUTH ADDITIONS

LOVE my enemies—use self-control
DO NOT speed over the limit
DO NOT vandalize
RESPECT authorities
NEVER eat on the subway
NEVER write on government property
NEVER kill
NEVER join a gang
NEVER be selfish
RESPECT your elders
NEVER blackmail (BULLYING)
NEVER have unprotected sex
NEVER betray your friends (BE A GOOD, TRUE FRIEND)

*Bracketed words added by POWELL HOUSE PROJECT 2009

**NEGATIVE RISK-TAKING (GAMBLING) DEFINED: Ask yourself the question, "DID SOMEONE ELSE HAVE TO LOSE IN ORDER FOR ME TO WIN?"

Powell House Project funded by the Department of Employment Services (DOES) and the DC Children and Youth Investment Trust Corporation (CYITC)

ADDITIONAL
MATERIALS

WOODSON QUOTES

from *The Mis-Education of the Negro* (1933)

"The problem of holding the Negro down, therefore, is easily solved. When you control a man's thinking you do not have to worry about his actions. You do not have to tell him not to stand here or go yonder. He will find his "proper place" and will stay in it. You do not need to send him to the back door. He will go without being told. In fact, if there is no back door, he will cut one for his special benefit. His education makes it necessary" (p. xiii).

"The same educational process which inspires and stimulates the oppressor with the thought that he is everything and has accomplished everything worthwhile, depresses and crushes at the same time the spark of genius in the Negro by making him feel that his race does not amount to much and never will measure up to the standards of other people" (p. xiii).

"History shows, then that as a result of these unusual forces in the education of the Negro he easily learns to follow the line of least resistance rather than battle against odds for what real history has shown to be the right course. A mind that remains in the present atmosphere never undergoes sufficient development to experience what is commonly known as thinking. No Negro thus submerged in the ghetto, then, will have a clear conception of the present status of the race or sufficient foresight to plan for the future; and he drifts so far toward compromise that he loses moral courage. The education of the Negro, then, becomes a perfect device for control from without. Those who purposely promote it have every reason to rejoice, and Negroes themselves exultingly champion the cause of the oppressor" (p. 54).

WOODSON QUOTES

from *The Mis-Education of the Negro* (1933)

"The lack of confidence of the Negro in himself and in his possibilities is what has kept him down. His mis-education has been a perfect success in this respect. Yet it is not necessary for the Negro to have more confidence in his own workers than in others. If the Negro would be as fair to his own as he has been to others, this would be all that is necessary to give him a new lease on life and start the trend upward" (p. 60).

"In our schools, and especially in schools of religion, attention should be given to the study of the Negro as he developed during the antebellum period by showing to what extent that remote culture was determined by ideas which the Negro brought with him from Africa. To take it for granted that the antebellum Negro was an ignoramus or that the native brought from Africa had not a valuable culture merely because some prejudiced writers have said so does not show the attitude of scholarship, and Negro students who direct their courses accordingly will never be able to grapple with the social problems presented today by the Negro church" (p. 81).

"The Association for the Study of Negro Life and History has no set solution to the problem of race except to learn to think" (p. 108).

"The mere imparting of information is not education. Above all things, the effort must result in making a man think and do for himself..." (p. xii).

Enslavement to Slavery to Freedom
As the Youth See It

Use this script to engage

audiences in your community

<h1 align="center">Characters</h1>

Student One
Student Two
Student Three
Student Four
Voice of Reason: Dr. Carter G. Woodson
W.E.B. DuBois
Booker T. Washington
William Monroe Trotter
Marcus Garvey
Ida B. Wells Barnett
Martin Luther King
Medgar Evers
Angela Davis

Setting: This play takes place in a fictitious, hopeful environment in 2005. The students' school system has recently announced the inclusion of African American history in the study of United States history. Four students have just received an assignment that requires them to research the arrival of the first people of African descent in what became known as the United States of America, and they also chart the enslavement, emancipation, and progress of Africans and African descended Americans in the United States.

Scene

Enslaved men and women are in the woods with Harriet Tubman, and they are escaping to freedom. They are following Tubman and taking in her every word.

NARRATOR

(Play "Love Ye One Another" on the Kiamsha CD "Pathways" while NARRATOR speaks)

In the catastrophic and chaotic perils of time, the spirit of the Lord would reveal to us that it is hard to send your love up to God, without sending your love out—to all mankind. For how can you love me, who you have not seen, but not love your brother, of whom you see daily? What you must understand, child of God, is that God is love. And he loved us so much that He gave his only begotten Son that whosoever would believe in Him would not perish, but have an everlasting life. And the apostle of the letter John encourages us, my beloved, to continue to love one another.

(HARRIET and SLAVES enter)

For the love is of God and everyone that loves is born of God and knoweth God. For a brother is born for adversity and a friend loveth at all times.

(fade song out during end of first verse)

HARRIET

(Immediately begin playing song "Pathways to Freedom." Play photo slideshow throughout entire song)

I seen the face of the slave owner and his whip.
I so despise the horrid crack of that whip.
It's the crack of sex as we breed like cattle
And lose our chil'un.
It's the crack of violence – we bleed so we make others bleed.
It's the crack of drugs drowning us in a drunken stupor simply because we hate who we are without it.
It's the crack of crack at the crack of dawn.
Our ancestors scream out emphatically it is time!
We must grab that whip and beat that slave owner until he breathes no more.

(Harriet rises up and looks and points upward)

Y'all see that house up yonder?
Ya can't see it so good now, but you can sees it better when we up and close in the dark morning.
That's that white lady house—she hides us by day and then she gives us a boat to cross the river to the next person's house to the next morning and next dark morning...til we ride that train to freedom!

SLAVES

Yeah!

(HARRIET and SLAVES exit stage)

NARRATOR

(Play Instrumental of "Love Ye One Another during NARRATOR'S statement)

The observance of Negro History Week, now celebrated as Black History Month, has proved to be one of the most fortunate steps ever taken by the Association for the Study of African

American Life and History, Incorporated. The celebration made a deep impression. It is a thought which emerged in 1926 from the mind of the director of the Association at the time, Dr. Carter Godwin Woodson, the Father of Black History. The main thought in establishing this observance cannot be better described than in the very words of Dr. Woodson.

VOICE OF REASON: DR. WOODSON
(Play "Rainbow of Love" Instrumental while Dr. Woodson speaks from backstage)
In ancient days, men had less race hate than we find today. The earliest historians recorded the achievements of all nations regardless of race or color. Even in the case of little contact, there was an effort to give honorable mention to all. Homer, for example, mentioned the Ethiopians as the "farthest removed of men." Herodotus said the Ethiopians feasted among the Gods. As kingdoms and empires developed around powerful dynasties, however, history tended to become self-glorification and an inculcation of national bias, race hate, and race prejudice. In the modern world we are the heirs of this incubus. Teachers of history, then, have been largely propagandists selecting those truths which stimulate these vicious tendencies and rejecting those which work to the contrary. The schools of America and Europe, therefore, have practically no conception of history. They have been so far misled by propaganda that actual history is branded as heresy.

<u>Scene</u>

Four students seated together at a table with lots of reference books, highlighters, pens, and research material all around them. There are posters on the wall depicting the Black history theme at the time. They discuss The Niagara Movement, W.E.B. DuBois, William Monroe Trotter, and Booker T. Washington, among others.

NARRATOR

Let's join four high school seniors who have, after four months of research, come together to put the finishing touches on a research assignment.

STUDENT ONE

It is so exciting that our school system has finally incorporated African American history into the history of America. This assignment *really* reflects this change.

STUDENT TWO

And, *The Mis-Education of the Negro* by Dr. Carter G. Woodson is now required reading. I enjoyed reading it last year as a junior. And this year, I can see how our assignments are helping us really get into the thinking of Dr. Woodson. You know, requiring us to re-read this book and connect quotes from Dr. Woodson's book with some of the historical events before and after the Niagara Movement was really an eye opener. There are so many profound statements made by Dr. Woodson, and it is unbelievable that Dr. Woodson made those statements so long ago because they really relate to everything that's going on today.

STUDENT ONE

I agree. If only people had listened then. (*Pause*) To be honest, we have to be careful and make sure we're really listening now! This Niagara Movement is nothing but the truth—the first national organization of African Americans—men at that—that aggressively and unconditionally demanded the same civil rights for their people which other Americans enjoyed. This research exercise really opened my eyes to so much history I was unaware of or just plain confused about. Now, let's look at each of our assignments:

Group One, you were to "Describe the key founders of the Niagara Movement, W.E.B. DuBois and William Monroe Trotter, and the ascendancy of the man this movement directly challenged, Booker T. Washington."

Group Two, your task was to "Describe and analyze the social changes in the United States from 1860 to 1910 and also analyze the Civil War and its connection to social change in the same period."

Group Three, "Describe the Birth of Jim Crow, the effects of Plessy v. Ferguson, the emergence of the NAACP, and major efforts to reform American society during that period."

Group Four, you were to "Visit each decade beginning with 1840 and record at least three significant events or prominent people in that timeframe, and examine the horror of mob-sanctioned murder orchestrated by lynching."

As it relates to the key founders of the Niagara Movement, I came across a monologue written by Dudley Randall of a conversation between W.E.B. DuBois and Booker T. Washington that explains their differences in opinion perfectly. I can just visualize them as Booker T says to W.E. B. "It seems to me . . .

BOOKER T. WASHINGTON
(*Spotlight on WASHINGTON at stage right.*)

It seems to me,
It shows a mighty lot of cheek
To study chemistry and Greek.
When Mister Charlie needs a hand,
To hoe the cotton on his land,
And when Miss Ann looks for a cook,
Why stick your nose inside a book?

W.E.B. DUBOIS
(*Spotlight on DUBOIS at stage left.*)

I don't agree,
If I should have the drive to seek
Knowledge of chemistry or Greek,
I'll do it. Charles and Miss can look
Another place for hand or cook,
Some men rejoice in skill of hand,
And some in cultivating land,
But there are others who maintain
The right to cultivate the brain.

BOOKER T. WASHINGTON
(*Spotlight on WASHINGTON at stage right.*)

It seems to me,
That all you folks have missed the boat
Who shout about the right to vote,
And spend vain days and sleepless nights
In uproar over civil rights.
Just keep your mouths shut, do not grouse,
But work, and save, and buy a house.

W.E.B. DUBOIS
(*Spotlight on DUBOIS at stage left.*)

I don't agree,
For what can property avail
If dignity and justice fail?
Unless you help to make the laws,
They'll steal your house with trumped-up clause.
A rope's as tight, a fire as hot,
No matter how much cash you've got.
Speak soft, and try your little plan,
But as for me, I'll be a man.

BOOKER T. WASHINGTON
(*Spotlight on WASHINGTON at stage right.*)

It seems to me....

W.E.B. DUBOIS
(Spotlight on DUBOIS at stage left.)

I don't agree.

STUDENT ONE

In a speech that Washington gave at the Atlanta Exposition on Sept. 18, 1885, he summarized, in one sentence, his concept of race relations appropriate for the times. In all things that are . . .
(STUDENT ONE voice fades out and BOOKER T. WASHINGTON comes in)

BOOKER T. WASHINGTON
(Voice of BOOKER T. WASHINGTON speaks from backstage. Display photo on screen in background)

In all things that are purely social we can be as separate as the fingers, yet one as the hand in all things essential to mutual progress.

STUDENT TWO

William Monroe Trotter, cofounder of the Niagara Movement with DuBois, had a similar background as DuBois, as they both grew up in privileged situations. He was actually the editor of a newspaper he founded, *The Guardian*, a Boston-based African American newspaper that challenged Booker T. Washington's philosophy of accommodation in the first half of the twentieth century. He and DuBois were Harvard educated and both believed strongly that they should demand what they knew they already deserved as American citizens. In 1903, Trotter interrupted a speech of Washington's; he was escorted out and jailed for one month at what was called the Boston Riot as he criticized the organization for being too controlled by white money and white leadership. Along with DuBois, Trotter drafted the Declaration of Principles:

WILLIAM MONROE TROTTER
(TROTTER comes out with paper and reads the introduction to principles)

We refuse to allow the impression to remain that the Negro-American assents to inferiority, is submissive under oppression, and apologetic before insults. We will not be satisfied to take one jot or tittle less than our full manhood rights. We claim for ourselves every single right that belongs to a freeborn American, political, civil and social; and until we get these rights we will never cease to protest and assail the ears of America. The battle we wage is not for ourselves alone but for all true Americans. It is a fight for ideals, lest this, our common fatherland, false to its founding, become in truth the land of the thief and the home of the slave—a byword and a hissing among the nations for its sounding pretensions and pitiful accomplishments.

VOICE OF REASON: DR. WOODSON
(Play "Rainbow of Love" instrumental while DR. WOODSON speaks from backstage)

If we would know history, we must not tarry too long with the exploits of Alexander the Great, the campaigns of Caesar, or the conquests of Napoleon. Warriors deserve attention as regimes to clear the way for the new, but these military chieftains were not intentionally great men. They aspired to be imposters, exploiters, and oppressors, rather than benefactors of humanity. We should record the achievements of men like Watts with the steam engine, Fulton with the steamboat, Morse with the telegraph, Bell with the telephone, Marconi with the wireless telegraph, Roentgen with the X-ray, Edison with the phonograph, and Matzliger with the lasting machine by which the shoe industry was revolutionized. We should exalt Socrates dying for the truth among the Greeks, St. Francis Assisi giving up all to help the poor, and Savonarola presenting himself as a living sacrifice for the faith. And we must not forget such reformers as Woolman, Benezet, Jefferson, Wilberforce, Cobden, Bright, Phillips, Douglass, Garrison, Sumner, Lovejoy, and Lincoln, who have illuminated the pages of modern history.

STUDENT ONE
Trotter's *Guardian* played a significant role in energizing DuBois, the Niagara Movement, and other anti-Washington forces.

STUDENT THREE
DuBois described his excitement about the first meeting.

W.E.B. DUBOIS
(DUBOIS stands stage left and says part)
Fifty-nine colored men from 17 different states eventually signed a call for a meeting near Buffalo, New York, during the week of July 9, 1905. I went to Buffalo and hired a little hotel on the Canadian side of the river at Fort Erie, and waited for the men to attend the meeting. If sufficient men had not come to pay for the hotel, I should certainly have been in bankruptcy and perhaps in jail; but as a matter of fact, 29 men, representing 14 states, came.

STUDENT THREE
Just look at the simplicity of the Declaration of Principles that Trotter and DuBois drafted as key issues addressed by the Niagara Men at their first meeting. These are rights that no one should have to beg for—they should be a given:

WILLIAM MONROE TROTTER
(TROTTER comes out with paper and reads the principles)
We congratulate the Negro-Americans on certain undoubted evidences of progress in the last decade, particularly the increase of intelligence, the buying of property, the checking of crime, the uplift in home life, the advance in literature and art, and the demonstration of constructive and executive ability in the conduct of great religious, economic and educational institutions. At the same time, we believe that this class of American citizens should protest emphatically and continually against the curtailment of their political rights. We believe in manhood suffrage; we believe that no man is so good, intelligent, or wealthy, as to be entrusted wholly with the welfare of his neighbor. So we declare this Declaration of Principles:

Number one, freedom of speech and criticism. Number two, an unfettered and unsubsidized press. We suggest that the press is bought and controlled and contend that we would remain a captive race unless our own propaganda reaches and arouses the people. Number three, manhood suffrage. We demand to participate in the American political system, North and South, on the same basis as whites. Number four, the abolition of all caste distinctions based simply on race and color. Racism was denounced as "unreasoning human savagery" and Jim Crow was condemned as an avenue for insult as well as "crucifixion of manhood." Number five, the recognition of the principles of human brotherhood as a practical present creed. DuBois considered that the Niagara Movement's task was to interpret the real Christ to white Christians. Number six, recognition of the highest and best human training is a monopoly of no class or race. The Niagara men believed in universal common school education. High school and technical high school were to be available to those "who wanted them." Number seven, a belief in the dignity of labor.

STUDENT FOUR

The Niagara Movement also asserted that Negroes must have equal employment opportunities. Employers and trade unions were severely criticized for racial discrimination. The denial of equal opportunities to us in economic life, this amounts to peonage which is denounced. And, last but not least, health, for an opportunity to live in decent houses and localities, for a chance to rear our children in physical and moral cleanliness.

STUDENT THREE

Can you believe such basic rights had to be fought for? We take so much for granted.

W.E.B. DUBOIS
(DUBOIS enters and stands stage left and says part)

We claim for ourselves every single right that belongs to a freeborn American, political, civil, and social; and until we get these rights we will never cease to protest and assail the ears of America!

STUDENT TWO
(Looks down as if reading)

Right along with the demands they were making, they also urged corresponding duties on their own people, as well, such as the duty to vote; the duty to respect the rights of others; the duty to work; the duty to obey the laws; the duty to be clean and orderly; the duty to send our children to school; the duty to respect ourselves, even as we respect others. This statement, complaint, and prayer we submit to the American people, and to Almighty God.

It's really sad that even today, it's still like pulling teeth to get people to go to the polls to vote, and many of our neighborhoods are disorderly. Our generation is dropping out of school, and we certainly have a lot of people not working, breaking the law, and disrespecting themselves and their elders. Wow, we're a mess! Let's see,
> *(Pause)*

Who is another significant character in the movement?

STUDENT ONE

You cannot talk about this movement without including discussion about Marcus Garvey. Although Garvey first had an interest in Washington's philosophy, he eventually came to believe that civil rights for African Americans would not happen without a fight. In his own words, Garvey said:

MARCUS GARVEY
(GARVEY reads from backstage. Display photo.)

I read of the conditions in America. I read *Up from Slavery* by Booker T. Washington, and then my doom—if I may so call it—of being a race leader dawned upon me in London after I had traveled through almost half of Europe. I asked, "Where is the black man's Government?" "Where is his King and his kingdom? "Where is his President, his country, and his ambassador, his army, his navy, his men of big affairs?" I could not find them, and then I declared. "I will help to make them." I was determined that the black man would not continue to be kicked about by all the other races and nations of the world, as I saw it in the West Indies, South and Central America and Europe, and as I read of it in America.
> *(Enters stage)*

My young and ambitious mind led me into flights of great imagination. I saw before me then, even as I do now, a new world of black men, not peons, serfs, dogs and slaves, but a nation of sturdy men making their impress upon civilization and causing a new light to dawn upon the human race. I could not remain in London any more. My brain was afire. There was a world of thought to conquer. I had to start ere it became too late and the work be not done. Immediately, I boarded a ship at Southampton for Jamaica, where I arrived on July 15, 1914. The Universal Negro Improvement Association and African Communities (Imperial) League was founded and organized five days after my arrival, with the program of uniting all the Negro peoples of the world into one great body to establish a country and Government absolutely their own. "As we pray to Almighty God to save us through his Holy Words so shall we with confidence in ourselves follow the sentiment of the Declaration of Rights and carve our way to liberty."

STUDENT FOUR

The Niagara Movement lasted only five short years because, eventually, DuBois and Trotter came into conflict, and Booker T. Washington, with his influence, undermined the movement. But the Niagara men laid the foundation for the National Association for the Advancement of Colored People (the NAACP). DuBois was one of the original leaders and founding members and was the first editor of *The Crisis*, the NAACP's magazine, which is still in existence today. Women were allowed to join the second year of the movement in1906 when they met at Harpers Ferry, Virginia, the site of John Brown's raid. Ida B. Wells Barnett was one of the players who joined the NAACP from the beginning on the urging of DuBois.

VOICE OF REASON: DR. WOODSON
(*Play "Rainbow of Love" Instrumental while DR. WOODSON speaks from backstage*)
We should especially emphasize the virtues of the heroes and heroines who, imbibing the spirit of the Great Nazarene, have suffered and died for ideals. As He died to make men holy, they call the roll of Daniel Drayton in the jail of the capital of the nation, L.W. Paine in the State prison in Georgia, Calvin Fairbank twice under such a sentence in Kentucky, and Andrew Torrey dying in the Maryland penitentiary, all merely because they helped the fugitive on the way to freedom. Among them we should give a high place of honor to Nat Turner who lived up to the ideal of Jesus that, "greater love hath no man than this, that a man lay down his life for his friends." And John Brown, inspired by the example of Nat Turner, would close the chapter with the moral courage and martyrdom, which made him one of the saints of God.

STUDENT THREE
Ida B. Wells-Barnett was a fearless anti-lynching crusader, women's rights advocate, journalist and speaker. She will be remembered as one of our nation's most uncompromising leaders and most ardent defenders of democracy. Although enslaved prior to the Civil War, she fought for racial and gender justice. In 1884, she was asked by the conductor of the Chesapeake & Ohio Railroad Company to give up her seat on the train to a white man and ordered her into the smoking or "Jim Crow" car. Despite the 1875 Civil Rights Act banning discrimination on the basis of race, creed, or color this was her experience:

IDA B. WELLS BARNETT
(*BARNETT reads from backstage. Display photo.*)
He tried to drag me out of the seat, but the moment he caught hold of my arm, I fastened my teeth in the back of his hand. I had braced my feet against the seat in front and was holding the back, and as he had already been badly bitten, he didn't try it again by himself. He went

forward and got the baggage man and another to help him, and of course, they succeeded in dragging me out, encouraged by white ladies and gentlemen in the car; some even stood on the seats so they could get a good view and continued applauding the conductor for his brave stand.

STUDENT FOUR
Mrs. Wells-Barnett took her case to court, and if that was not bad enough, the justice system let her down, as well.

IDA B. WELLS BARNETT
(BARNETT reads from backstage. Display photo.)
I felt so disappointed because I had hoped such great things from my suit for my people, generally. I have firmly believed all along that the law was on our side and would, when we appealed to it, give us justice. I feel shorn of that belief and utterly discouraged, and just now, if it were possible, would gather my race in my arms and fly away with them.

STUDENT FOUR
In 1892, she experienced the lynching of three of her friends who were owners of a local grocery store. A group of angry, white men thought they would eliminate the competition, but her friends fought back by shooting one of the attackers. An angry lynch mob broke into the jail, dragged them away from town, and brutally murdered all three.

STUDENT ONE
Commenting on this incident, Wells-Barnett wrote, "The city of Memphis has demonstrated that neither character nor standing avails the Negro if he dares to protect himself against the white man." Although Ida B. Wells-Barnett moved to Chicago after her newspaper office was destroyed, through her writings, she continued her blistering attacks on Southern injustices.

IDA B. WELLS BARNETT
(On Stage)
Let us remember and constantly recall to the minds of the civilized world the fact that this nation which declares that "all men are created free and equal" still continues to violate its own professed principles and written laws.

ACT THREE [Corresponds with Lesson Three in Curriculum Section]

<u>Scene</u>

The four students are still seated at the table. They discuss social changes in the United States from 1860 to 1910.

STUDENT TWO

Our task was to: "Describe and analyze the social changes in the United States from 1860 to 1910." Analyze the Civil War and its connection to social change in the same period. After analyzing the events that took place during and after the Civil War, the Niagara Movement was necessary in the life of African Americans. I learned that in the 1840s and 50s, the Northern states wanted to prohibit slavery in the Western territories that would eventually become new states. The Southern states opposed all efforts to block the expansion of slavery and feared that the North's stance would eventually endanger existing slaveholdings in the South itself.

STUDENT THREE

By the1850s, some Northerners had begun calling for the complete abolition of slavery, while several Southern states threatened to secede from the Union as a means to protect their right to keep slaves.

STUDENT TWO

And that is exactly what happened. When Abraham Lincoln, the candidate of the antislavery Republican Party, was elected president in late 1860, the Southern states carried out their threat and seceded.

VOICE OF REASON: DR. WOODSON

(*Play "Rainbow of Love" Instrumental while DR. WOODSON speaks from backstage*)

This is the meaning of Negro History Week. It is not so much a Negro History Week as it is a History Week. We should emphasize not Negro History, but the Negro in history. What we need is not history of selected races or nations, but the history of the world void of national bias, race hate, and religious prejudice. There should be no indulgence in undue eulogy of the Negro. The case of the Negro is well taken care of when it is shown how he has influenced the development of civilization.

The fact is, however, that one race has not accomplished any more good than any other race, for God could not be just and at the same time make one race the inferior of the other. But if you leave it to the one to set forth his own virtues while disparaging those of others, it will not require many generations before all credit for human achievements will be ascribed to one particular stock. Such is the history taught the youth today.

STUDENT ONE

Wait a minute, Abraham Lincoln, an antislavery Republican? So, Blacks were voting Republican in those days? When did that change? And it's really hard to believe, that was also during the time that Howard University was founded—yeh 1867 to be exact.

STUDENT THREE

Well ,that is really a part of the social change—I was really shocked to learn these facts. Angry Southerners from the states of the former Confederacy enacted the Black Codes immediately after the American Civil War. Black Codes were designed to assure the continuance of white supremacy and replace the social controls of slavery that had been removed by the Emancipation Proclamation and the Thirteenth Amendment to the Constitution. They were based on the concept that slaves were property, not persons, and that the law must protect not only the property but also the property owner from the danger of violence.

STUDENT FOUR

Right, the Black Codes had their root in the slave codes that had formerly been in effect. The general philosophy supporting the institution of chattel slavery in America was, slave rebellions were not unknown and the possibility of uprisings, so they enacted the black codes. Believe it or not, the Democratic Party did not rally enough support until the New Deal era during the Depression of the 1930s to place Franklin D. Roosevelt in office in 1932.

STUDENT ONE

And even through Reconstruction, 1865 through 1877, attempts were made to solve the political, social, and economic problems arising from the readmission to the Union of the eleven Confederate states that had seceded at or before the outbreak of war.

The Thirteenth, Fourteenth, and Fifteenth Constitutional Amendments were intended to ensure civil rights of the freedmen signed into law. Southerners particularly resented the activities of the Freedmen's Bureau, which Congress had established to feed, protect, and help educate the newly emancipated blacks. Believe it or not, Black Codes, Jim Crow, and the Ku Klux Klan were all established as a direct result of the new freedom the enslaved persons found. The Southerners just would not accept such freedom for Blacks.

<u>Scene</u>
The four students are still seated at the table. They discuss briefly Jim Crow, Plessy v. Ferguson, the NAACP, and reform.

STUDENT TWO
So let's look at the next group assignment which is to: "Describe the Birth of Jim Crow, Plessy v. Ferguson, the emergence of the NAACP, and Major Efforts to Reform American Society" during that period. Plessy v. Ferguson, passed in 1896, said that Jim Crow laws are constitutional under the doctrine of "Separate but Equal." Police arrested Homer Plessy for refusing to leave a railroad car that prohibited "colored" people. Under Louisiana law, Plessy was "colored" because he was one-eighth black. The Court ruled that the race-based Jim Crow laws did not violate the Constitution as long as the states proffered separate but equal treatment. Believe it or not, Jim Crow laws were not ultimately defeated until 1954 when the Brown v. Board of Education case was won.

STUDENT ONE
How in the world could such laws that enforced racial segregation in the U.S. South not only be put into place but last between the end the formal Reconstruction period in 1877 and the beginning of a strong Civil Rights Movement in the1950s? That's absolutely unbelievable to me!

Oh, I really, really get the picture now. The Niagara Movement was just the initial step in obtaining equality for all. Radical was just what was needed. The Niagara Movement met annually until 1910 when DuBois called for its members to join the NAACP. With the financial backing and social influence of its white members, the NAACP was able to accomplish many of the long-term goals the Niagara movement had set out to achieve. The NAACP would soon become one of the most formidable and successful civil rights organizations in the nation.
(*Everyone Shakes heads in agreement*)

STUDENT TWO
Last, but not least, our assignment directs us to visit each decade from 1840 to present and record at least three significant events or prominent people in that timeframe and examine the horror of mob-sanctioned murder orchestrated by lynching. I was actually dumbfounded to discover so much research, scientific research, has been done to get into the minds of lynch mobs. This is an atrocity that, as a nation, places an indelible mark on our history. I found a great quote from Henry McNeal Turner's *Twentieth Century Negro Literature or a Cyclopedia of Thought on the Vital Topics Relating to the American Negro,* published in 1902:

"No savage nation can exceed the atrocities which are often heralded through the country and accepted by many as an incidental consequence. Men are hung, shot, and burnt by bands of murderers who are most invariable represented as the most influential and respectable citizens, while the evidence of guilt of what is charged against the victims is never established in any court."

Also, in an article written by Dr. Ida E. Jones in a recent *Black History Bulletin,* she explored how lynch mobs sometimes used religion to justify lynching. Dr. Jones stated:

"The use of religion as a hierarchy and impetus is believed to be the drive behind many lynchings. The order of leadership is implicit in lynch mobs. There is a core of leaders who rally others to action in orderly and directed fashion. There is no division between the followers and the objective is clearly defined and pursued. The area of impetus is derived from the moral justice lynch mobs thought they were creating. They were righting the wrongs a community faced by select individuals."

VOICE OF REASON: DR. WOODSON
(*Play "Rainbow of Love" Instrumental while DR. WOODSON speaks from backstage*)
Let the light of history enable us to see that "enough of good there is in the lowest estate to sweeten life; enough of evil in the highest to check presumption; enough there is of both in all estates to bind us in compassionate brotherhood, to teach us impressively that we are of one dying and one immortal family." Let truth destroy the dividing prejudices of nationality and teach universal love without distinction of race, merit or rank. With the sublime enthusiasm and heavenly vision of the Great Teacher let us help men to rise above the race hate of this age unto the altruism of a rejuvenated universe.

STUDENT FOUR
Whoa, Whoa, Whoa . . . this is very, very insightful. As we look at the many hundreds, in fact thousands, of lynchings that took place from 1870 to 1933 because reports were well documented on each lynch case from early on, it brings to bear two very important matters that we as youth are faced with today. Dr. Jones analyzed the use of religion and the order of leadership, and it brought to mind peer pressure among youth today and the order of leadership among teenagers. With our peers, the impetus is derived from our desire to be included so we present no division between the follower and the leader: Peer Pressure. So we engage in drugs, pre-marital sexual activity, skipping school, and disobedience to our parents, things that, if led to decide alone, we might never do, just to right the wrong of not being accepted by our peers.

STUDENT THREE
That is very, very deep, and it brings to mind a quote by Dr. Woodson that I also ran across in my research in a *Black History Bulletin* when he said:
(*Play "Rainbow of Love" Instrumental while DR. WOODSON speaks from backstage*)
As another has well said, to handicap a student by teaching him that his black face is a curse and that his struggle to change his condition is hopeless is the worst sort of lynching. It kills one's aspirations and dooms him to vagabondage and crime. It is strange, then, that the friends of truth and the promoters of freedom have not risen up against the present propaganda in the schools and crushed it. This crusade is much more important than the anti-lynching movement, because there would be no lynching if it did not start in the schoolroom. Why not exploit, enslave, or exterminate a class that everybody is taught to regard as inferior.

ACT FIVE [Corresponds with Lesson Five in Curriculum Section]

Scene

The four students are still seated at the table. They discuss the decade research portion of their assignment.

STUDENT TWO

Now I see why we had to look at the 100 years before and after Niagara. This assignment really made us *think* critically! As we look at decade after decade to explore not only the atrocities but also the successes taking place, we must take the time to see where we intend to take this history in the next l00 years. It is our responsibility, you know. Okay, now let's discuss the decades.
(Looks down at book for information)
Let's see, it says here that in 1895, 105 blacks were lynched.

STUDENT FOUR

You know, Charles Chesnutt published his book.

STUDENT THREE

(Looks at notes on paper)
And I have that *Up From Slavery: An Autobiography* was published.

STUDENT ONE

Oh, and I have, the last African American leaves Congress.

STUDENT TWO

Okay, now let's look at 1900 to 1909.
(Pauses to read notes)
Wow. It says here that 106 blacks were lynched in 1900.

STUDENT ONE

And during this decade, there were three race riots. There was one in New York, where police brutality attacked the Black community. There was a riot in Atlanta that was sensationalized by a reporting of a "crime wave" of rapes and murders by Blacks. Then, there were brutal attacks on Blacks in Illinois where Blacks were used as strike breakers.

STUDENT THREE

Well, you know what, I have some good news. John Hope became the president of Morehouse College.

STUDENT FOUR

And, the NAACP, the National Association for the Advancement of Colored People, was founded in New York, with its focus on civil rights. And we know we want that.

STUDENT THREE

That's right.

STUDENT TWO

Now, let's discuss 1910 through 1919.
(Pauses to read notes)

Well, dag! It says that during this time period over 588 Blacks were lynched.

STUDENT FOUR
Oh my goodness! Well, here's something positive. Dr. Carter G. Woodson founded the Association for the Study of Negro Life and History in 1915.

STUDENT ONE
I found something. The United States entered World War I. Unfortunately, Blacks were segregated in the military.

STUDENT THREE
I found something, too. The first Pan African Congress was organized by W.E.B. DuBois. The convention was held in Paris, France.

STUDENT ONE
Okay, now let's look at the next decade, 1920 to 1929. It says here that in 1920, alone, there were 150 lynchings. In one year!

STUDENT THREE
Wow. That's ridiculous.

STUDENT ONE
I have some news about the successes of our people. Did you know that from 1920 to 1929, there were over 70,000 Blacks engaged in business? That seems like more than today.

STUDENT TWO
That's incredible. Oooh. You know what else happened during this period? The Harlem Renaissance, Black creativity in the nation's largest Black community, with entertainers, and artists, and poets, everybody, just showing all of their talents.

STUDENT FOUR
And Carter G. Woodson started Negro History Week, which later turned into Black History Month.

VOICE OF REASON: DR. WOODSON
(Play "Rainbow of Love" Instrumental while Dr. Woodson speaks from backstage)
On the other hand, just as thorough education in the belief in the equality of races has brought the world to the cat-and-dog stage of religious and racial strife, so may thorough instruction in the equality of races bring about a reign of brotherhood through an appreciation of the virtues of all races, creeds and colors. In such a millennium the achievements of the Negro properly set forth will crown him as a factor in early human progress and a maker of modern civilization. He has supplied the demand for labor of a large area of our country, he has been a conservative force in its recent economic development; he has given the nation a poetic stimulus; he has developed the most popular music of the modern era; and he has preserved in its purity the brotherhood taught by Jesus of Nazareth. In his native country, moreover, he produced in the ancient world a civilization contemporaneous with that of the nations of the early Mediterranean, he influenced the cultures then cast in the crucible of time, and he taught the modern world the use of iron by which science and initiative have remade the universe. Must we let this generation continue ignorant of these eloquent facts?

STUDENT TWO

Okay, so let's go to 1930 through 1939. Let's see . . .
(Pauses)
Anybody find one . . .?

STUDENT FOUR

OOO, I have one, the National Council of Negro Women was organized by Mary McLeod Bethune to fight racial and gender discrimination.

STUDENT ONE

I found one, the National Negro Congress organized over 800 delegates from more than 500 organizations.

STUDENT THREE

Joe Louis, you know that's my boxing man right there, he became the heavy weight champion of the world. And at the Olympics, Black athletes won 13 gold medals in Germany. Thirteen!

STUDENT TWO

Okay, here's one. It says that the opera singer, Marion Anderson, was not allowed to sing at Constitution Hall in Washington, D.C. by the Daughters of the American Revolution, but she did get to sing at the Lincoln Memorial in front of 75,000 people.

STUDENT ONE

The fifth decade from 1940 to 1949, let's see if we can find something.

STUDENT TWO

Well, here's one...it says...wait a minute—it says over five anti-lynching bills were introduced in the 77th Congress, but none of them were passed. That's crazy!

STUDENT ONE

That is crazy, and listen to this, listen to this, going back to our armed forces—Blacks were finally allowed to enlist in the United States Navy, but the Navy had a quota system for the number of blacks that were allowed to join.

STUDENT FOUR

I found a good one though. There were 11 Black banks with deposits amounting to over $14 million dollars.

STUDENT ONE

That was like 14 trillion dollars back then...
(Everyone laughs)

STUDENT THREE

That's a whole lot of money—a whole lot of money. But the Tuskegee Airmen escorted allied planes and bombers in World War II, and they never lost a bomber to enemy fire. That's positive—that's good.

STUDENT TWO

What about 1950 –to 1959

STUDENT THREE

Let's see . . . Oh, another boxing man—that's my man—Sugar Ray Robinson won the welter weight and the middle weight championship titles.

STUDENT FOUR

This one. I found one that is really important: the U.S. Supreme Court rules against racial discrimination and segregation in the Brown v. Board of Education case. You know what, this was last year's Black history month theme in celebration of the fiftieth anniversary of the court case. Thurgood Marshall and Charles Houston were very important, too.

STUDENT ONE

I found one. W.E.B. DuBois identified with pro-Russian causes. He was indicted in 1951 as an unregistered agent for a foreign power. He was acquitted by a federal judge, but at the same time, DuBois, by the time it was all over, and I can't blame him, he had become completely disillusioned with the United States. Hmm. Wow.

STUDENT TWO

It says here that Nat King Cole had his first national television variety show and good old Motown Records was founded by Barry Gordy, Jr.

STUDENT FOUR

Ooo, I found one. The Alvin Ailey American Dance Theatre was formed during this decade, also.

STUDENT TWO

Aren't they still around today? Okay, so let's see . . . let's go with 1960 to 1969.

STUDENT ONE

I found one, the Albany Movement, which constructed several civil rights organizations such as SCLC, SNCC, CORE, and the NAACP. They all joined forces to protest against discrimination in all public facilities, and, of course, local police responded with violence against demonstrators, whom we all have come to learn during this research were, of course, non-violent.

STUDENT THREE

Well, unfortunately, during this decade there were a lot of church bombings and burnings. You know, four little girls were killed at the Sixteenth Street Baptist Church when that was bombed.

STUDENT FOUR

What! In 1961 DuBois joined the Communist Party.

STUDENT TWO

Ok, I have one. It says the Turner Commission reported our nation as moving towards two separate societies—one Black—one White—separate and unequal—White racism is the primary cause of all of that.
(Pauses and searches for another answer)
Okay, here's another one. During this . . . this is the time when Medgar Evers was murdered. You know, Medgar Evers is one of the first willing victims of the Civil Rights movement. They said that in 1954 Medgar Evers became the first field secretary of the NAACP in Mississippi. He was outspoken and his demands were radical for his strictly segregated state. It says here he fought for the enforcement of the 1954 court decision of Brown v. Board of Education of

Topeka Kansas, which outlawed school segregation. He fought for the right to vote, and he advocated boycotting merchants who discriminated against others. He worked nonstop despite the threats of violence that his speeches created. He gave much of himself to this struggle, and in 1963, he gave his life. After his death, people became outraged and results were seen quickly. So many people began to get involved in politics and lobbying for equal rights. When Medgar Evers died in 1963, only 28,000 Blacks were registered to vote, but by 1971, there were 250,000. And by 1982, there were 500,000 Blacks registered to vote.

STUDENT THREE

You know, I read about that, too. Immediately after Evers's death, the shotgun that was used to kill him was found in bushes nearby, with the owner's fingerprints still fresh. Byron de la Beckwith, a vocal member of a local white-supremacist group, was arrested. Despite the evidence against him, including an earlier statement that he wanted to kill Evers, two trials with all-white juries ended in deadlock decisions and Beckwith went free. Twenty years later in 1989, information surfaced that suggested the jury in both trials had been tampered with. The assistant District Attorney, with the help of Evers' widow, began putting together a new case. On February 5, 1994, a multiracial jury re-tried Beckwith and found him guilty of the crime. He was sentenced to life in prison. And there's more . . . In December 2004 the airport in Jackson, Mississippi was named for Medgar Evers . . . Evers' legacy has come full circle.

MEDGAR EVERS
(EVERS speaks from backstage. Display photo.)
It may sound funny, but I love the South. I don't choose to live anywhere else. There's land here, where a man can raise cattle, and I'm going to do it someday. There are lakes where a man can sink a hook and fight the bass. There is room here for my children to play and grow, and become good citizens—if the white man will let them.

STUDENT THREE
The Civil Rights Act was passed by Congress. This act prohibited discrimination in public accommodations and employment.

MEDGAR EVERS
(Speaks from backstage)
You can kill a man but you can't kill an idea.

STUDENT TWO
Voting Rights Act Passed by Congress to enforce the 15th amendment to the Constitution of the United States and for other purposes.

MEGAR EVERS
(EVERS speaks from backstage. Display photo.)
Our only hope is to control the vote.

STUDENT ONE
And also during that decade, unfortunately, Dr. Martin Luther King was assassinated in April of 1968. There was a lot of Black rioting in major cities because of that, and after he died, there was no more Civil Rights Movement. The leadership split up and went their separate ways.

MARTIN LUTHER KING
(*KING speaks from backstage. Display photo.*)
We have no alternative but to protest. For many years, we have shown an amazing patience. We have sometimes given our White brothers the feeling that we liked the way we were being treated. But we come here tonight to be saved from that patience that makes us patient with anything less than freedom and justice.

STUDENT ONE
As Dr. King has said, "Injustice anywhere is a threat to justice everywhere."

MARTIN LUTHER KING
(*Display photo. KING speaks from backstage*)
You may well ask: "Why direct action?" Why sit-ins, marches and so forth: Isn't negotiation a better path? You are quite right in calling for negotiation. Indeed, this is the very purpose of direct action. Nonviolent direct action seeks to create such a crisis and foster such a tension that a community which has constantly refused to negotiate is forced to confront the issue. It seeks so to dramatize the issue that it can no longer be ignored. We know through painful experience that freedom is never voluntarily given by the oppressor; it must be demanded by the oppressed.

STUDENT ONE
You know what else happened in this decade? Thurgood Marshall was the first Black appointed to the United States Supreme Court.

THURGOOD MARSHALL
(*MARSHALL speaks from backstage. Display photo.*)
I do not believe that the meaning of the Constitution was forever fixed at the Philadelphia convention. The true miracle was not the birth of the Constitution, but its life, a life nurtured through two turbulent centuries of our own making.

STUDENT TWO
That's an important one. Okay, now let's look at 1970 to 1979. Oh my goodness, *Essence* magazine was published to highlight the beauty and achievements of Black women. I still get the *Essence* in my house today.

STUDENT ONE
And you know what else—the *Flip Wilson Show*, a variety television program, aired on prime time.

STUDENT THREE
I found one, too. The Tuskegee experiment was exposed after 40 years of Blacks being used as victims in a government study where over 300 Blacks were injected with syphilis and not given a cure.

STUDENT FOUR
I got one, too, Angela Davis is acquitted of conspiracy to kidnap and murder.

ANGELA DAVIS
(*DAVIS speaks from backstage. Display photo.*)
My thoughts are clear and my anger intense. Most of the issues that I raise find their roots in the hypocrisy of government and the blind greed of business. For example, I fiercely dissect the War on Drugs. For the most part, political speech of this sort is suppressed in the mainstream media. My central concern is with the U.S. (in)justice system. As citizens of the new electronic frontier, we take many freedoms for granted, but back in the physical realm the system is still corrupt. Politicians still flex their muscles at the expense of millions of innocents, and money still rest in the hands of the few. No matter how safe you may feel from persecution, it will eventually come knocking at your door. Let your struggle against it begin today.

STUDENT TWO
Okay, now let's talk about 1980 to 1989. Oh, here's a good one, Black Entertainment Television (BET) was founded by Robert L. Johnson, also known as Bob Johnson.

STUDENT ONE
Okay, on top of BET, we have to give props to Howard University who broadcasts its own television station WHMM.

STUDENT FOUR
And, in this decade, Black mayors increase in major cities.

STUDENT THREE
Also, Bill and Camille Cosby gave a generous, very generous, 20 million dollar gift to Spelman College.

STUDENT FOUR
Let's look at 1990 to 1999. Black actors and actresses receive eleven Emmy awards during this period.

STUDENT TWO
It says here that the Supreme Court ruled that the Ku Klux Klan has a right to burn crosses and is protected by the First amendment to the Constitution. Now, that's crazy.

STUDENT ONE
True, but on a positive note, Carol Mosley Braun was the first Black woman ever elected to the U.S. Senate.

STUDENT THREE
The survivors of the Rosewood massacre were awarded compensation for the 1923 White rampage of a Black community, killing Blacks and burning down their homes. I mean, that's like 70 years!

STUDENT ONE
Here's another good one, President Clinton established an advisory board on race.

STUDENT FOUR

Okay, 2000 to 2005. We're getting to the good stuff here. Kiamsha wins the Stop Racism Youth Challenge Award sponsored by the YWCAs of the United States and Canada by submitting their Modern-day UGRR Concept and Song entitled "Rainbow of Love" as a solution to the race problem.

STUDENT ONE

And, you know, although that was really positive, we can't talk about this decade without acknowledging the horrible attacks of September 11. These attacks were on the World Trade Center in New York City, both of the towers, and the Pentagon in Washington, D.C.

STUDENT THREE

On May 17, 2004, at a Brown v. Board of Education anniversary celebration, Bill Cosby made profound statements that made the Black community look into the mirror to check its stance and irresponsibility toward our families and children.

STUDENT ONE

You know, I'm really tempted to go and visit the recent statements made by Dr. Cosby. Basically, they are pointing at the youth today, at us, you know. It addressed what we are doing and not doing to take responsibility in society.
(Looks at STUDENT TWO)
Don't you have that article?

STUDENT TWO

(Reads paper)
"The lower economic people are not holding up their end in this deal. These people are not parenting."

STUDENT FOUR

(Interrupts)
See, I don't agree with him already!

STUDENT TWO

Wait a minute! Hear this out! "They are buying things for their kids, $500 sneakers for what? And won't spend $200 for Hooked on Phonics!"

"The enemy is us. There is a time, ladies and gentlemen when we have to turn the mirror around. I am critiquing all Blacks, not just the 50 percent of African Americans in the lower economic neighborhood who drop out of school and the alarming proportions of Black men in prison and Black teenage mothers."

To critics whose position is that it's unproductive to air our dirty laundry in public, Mr. Cosby responds,
"Your dirty laundry gets out of school at 2:30 every day. It's cursing on the way home, on the bus, train, in the candy store. They are cursing and grabbing each other and going nowhere. And, the book bag is very, very thin because there's nothing in it. Don't worry about the White man. I couldn't care less about what White people think about me . . . let em' talk. What are they saying that is different from what their grandfathers said and did to us? What is different is what we are doing to ourselves. We're going to turn that mirror around. It's not just the

poor—everybody's guilty. Before you get to the point where you say I can't do anything with them, do something with them, like:

Teach our children to speak English.

When the teacher calls, show up at the school.

When the idiot box starts spewing profane rap videos, turn it off.

Refrain from cursing around the kids.

Teach our boys that women should be cherished, not raped and demeaned.

Tell them that education is a prize we won with blood and tears, not a dishonor.

Stop making excuses for the agents and abettors of Black-on-Black crime.

It costs us nothing to do these things. But if we don't it will cost us infinitely more tears."

<u>Scene</u>
Still seated at the table, students wrap up their discussion and begin plotting a solution for the future.

VOICE OF REASON: DR. WOODSON
(*Play "Rainbow of Love" Instrumental while DR. WOODSON SPEAKS from backstage*)
The world does not want and will never have the heroes and heroines of the past. What this age needs is an enlightened youth not to undertake the tasks like theirs, but to imbibe the spirit of the great men and answer the present call to duty with equal nobleness of soul.

STUDENT ONE
You know, the enemy is us! Wisdom has been shared with us from Harriet Tubman, to Frederick Douglass, to Booker T. Washington, to W.E.B. DuBois, to Carter G. Woodson, to Martin Luther King, Jr., to your grandma and granddad, my grandma and granddad, and so, and so on, and so on. If we are not doing well in school, we're not doing our part, just as Mr. Cosby said. If we are not putting forth our best efforts and encouraging our peers to put forth their best effort, we're not doing our part.

STUDENT TWO
If we're not representing our people in public with attitudes and actions that represent our families with a sense of pride and respect, we're not doing our part. This history research project has really opened our eyes to see our role in all of this.

STUDENT FOUR
Even Frederick Douglass' answer, as early as 1895, to what had to be done to finally secure freedom was, "Agitate! Agitate! Agitate!" As our history proves, we have agitated for many, many years, and it was the necessary formula then. And because of our forefathers' diligence in bringing us to this point, our task will be accomplished by applying another method that was used alongside the method of agitation: "Apply Love, With More Love, And More Love."

STUDENT THREE
Knowing the truth about our history is so, so important. I never thought that examining the history of lynching would bring us to a need to share more love among each other. Hate is what got us where we are today. More of that would certainly destroy us! In fact, that reminds me of another quote from Dr. Woodson:

VOICE OF REASON: DR. WOODSON
(*Play "Rainbow of Love" Instrumental while DR. WOODSON speaks from backstage*)
In this outline there nothing to engender race hate. The Association does not bring out such publications. The aim of this organization is to set forth facts in scientific form, for facts properly set forth will tell their own story. No advantage can be gained by merely inflaming the Negro's mind against his traducers.

STUDENT TWO
We will accomplish racial harmony and true equality for all by applying *truth* to the void of misunderstanding and lack of knowledge, and begin to "Love One Another Just as God has

Loved Us." We must develop all the qualities of life so when negative comes our way, we will be able to take that negative incident as an opportunity to *teach* that person who is still in ignorance a better way, by activating self-control, patience, longsuffering, peace, joy . . . you get the message. This is a new day! We will enact an old method that is again the answer for accomplishing a new, necessary result. We will have to *make drastic changes in educating* our generation to prepare them to lead the next generation. The truth, the whole truth, and nothing but the truth is a necessary part of our solution.

STUDENT TWO:
Let's join the troops as we begin today, to help descendants of our heroes and heroines of the past secure the knowledge of our history to past it on to the next generation.

All agree with headshakes and comments.

THE END

(Optional Extended Scene)
Drill Sergeant and cadets are outside as cadets undergo training.

DRILL SERGEANT
(Drill Sergeant enters stage first)
MARCH!
(Soldiers march in)
HALT!
(Soldiers stop)
PRESENT ARMS!
(Soldiers pull out pencil and small notebook)
You are all here for a central cause. We have a battle to fight, and it is my job to train a willing and able group of soldiers. You have learned some very valuable information, and I want to make sure you remember it. The battle will not be an easy one, but we have identified ignorance as the problem and knowledge as our weapon. Private Barnett, Ida B. Wells-Barnett fervently fought against lynching and other violent crimes against African Americans, and she fought for gender equality. What were the strategies of resistance to racism that Wells-Barnett adopted, and how are those strategies relevant to our struggle today?

PRIVATE BARNETT
Ida B. Wells-Barnett risked her life and employment by speaking out against lynching and violence towards Blacks. She exhibited determination, courage, love, peace, goodness, and longsuffering; the qualities of life are still key to our struggle for racial equality.

DRILL SERGEANT
Medgar Evers, known as the first martyr of the Civil Rights movement, contributed to the movement with his death as well as his life. Private Evers, how is this so?

PRIVATE EVERS
Medgar Evers' assassination lifted the Civil Rights leader and WWII veteran to national attention. The heartless act of his killer angered many people in Mississippi and across the nation who shared Evers' cause. Evers' death effected change on a national level, prompting President Kennedy to ask Congress for a Civil Rights bill.

DRILL SERGEANT

Private King. Rev. Dr. Martin Luther King, Jr. is maybe the most prominent figure of the Civil Rights movement. His leadership, vision, and accomplishments are admired around the world. He, like Medgar Evers and many others, lost his life fighting for civil rights. Even so, his character has been criticized and attacked in recent years. How does hearing the reputation of such a celebrated Civil Rights figure being tarnished affect you, soldier.

PRIVATE KING

Martin Luther King, Jr. is one of my personal heroes. The first time I heard anything bad about him was in a movie. I couldn't believe it, I wouldn't believe it. Then, I decided to do some reading, and I found out that Dr. King wasn't perfect. But he was my hero because of the good that he did and the good that he stood for. And just because he may have done something that I didn't agree with, that doesn't nullify the good that he did for me and so many others.

DRILL SERGEANT

Private Garvey, we know that for a time, Marcus Garvey admired Booker T. Washington's philosophy of racial uplift through industrial training, but what prompted Garvey to take a more radical approach to opposing racial and political injustice?

PRIVATE GARVEY

Marcus Garvey and Booker T. Washington believed that Blacks should demonstrate good morals and strong character and that the majority would eventually acknowledge Blacks as equals. But when Garvey saw that Blacks fighting in WWI did not change the way Whites viewed Blacks, he realized that the majority would not give up equal rights without a fight.

DRILL SERGEANT

Private Washington and Private Dubois, Booker T. Washington and W.E.B. DuBois were both leaders of movements that sought racial harmony and social progress of Black Americans. Booker T. Washington served as an advisor to President Theodore Roosevelt and was the first Black man to dine at the White House, and W.E.B. DuBois was the first Black man to earn a PhD from Harvard. Though both were extremely accomplished in their own rights and dedicated to their missions of improving the condition of Black Americans, they differed in their approaches. Private DuBois, how did W.E.B DuBois' approach to achieving social progress differ from that of Washington's?

PRIVATE DUBOIS

W.E.B. DuBois felt that Washington's methods were appeasing to Whites and failed to achieve equality for Blacks. Therefore, DuBois helped found the radical Niagara Movement that demanded total racial equality and nothing less.

DRILL SERGEANT

Private Washington, though these two leaders began their undergraduate careers at two different institutions, which prepared them both to go on to have involved careers in academia, what similarities about these institutions jump out at you?

PRIVATE WASHINGTON

Booker T. Washington attended Hampton University and W.E.B. Dubois attended Fisk. Both of these are what we call Historically Black Colleges and Universities, and they are still cultivating Black leaders today.

DRILL SERGEANT

Private Trotter, William Monroe Trotter was the founder of *The Guardian,* a Boston newspaper dedicated to the fight against racial discrimination. Trotter targeted Booker T. Washington in this newspaper because he believed Blacks needed to lead, not accommodate. How did Trotter's radical views affect the Niagara Movement, and how did the results act as a catalyst for future movements?

PRIVATE TROTTER

William Trotter wanted a society in which Blacks would demand that White Americans give them rights. DuBois' views were similar, but DuBois wanted to be more inclusive of Whites in the movement, so over time they grew apart. The Niagara movement fell apart, and the NAACP was later formed to carry out its mission. Movements after the Niagara movement fell apart for similar reasons. Black people just had a hard time coming together without fighting amongst themselves.

DRILL SERGEANT

Private Tubman, Harriett Tubman, most commonly known for her quest on the Underground Railroad, led several hundred people to freedom. It is said that she never lost a single passenger. What can we learn from her determination to create change?

PRIVATE TUBMAN

Ummm….. Ummmmmm.

DRILL SERGEANT

Everyone write this down! Similar to our enslaved ancestors, we are becoming slaves to modern-day slave masters such as drugs, violence, premarital sex, and racial disharmony. To fight these enemies we must use weapons such as convictions, qualities of life, and absolute truth. This is why we are training you!! This is what we are teaching you! Our goal is to provide you with the proper weapons so you will learn how to think!

PRIVATE TUBMAN

Uhhh, Sir, can you repeat that please. I didn't quite get all of that.
(*Drill Sergeant shakes his head*)

DRILL SERGEANT

Just remember that battles will always occur. That never changes, but the way you fight them should.

Scene 2
Peek into the Future: Fifty Years Later

Inside a classroom, there are computers and flags of different countries on the wall. There are different races of students in the room and all are looking on the computer screen for their lesson. Their dress is a little weird compared to the tastes of the current generation. The students are sitting and listening intensely as the teacher is teaching on the Civil Rights Movement.

TEACHER

So to conclude our lesson for today, what impact did Medgar Evers have on society during the 1960s?
(*Students call out different answers in Unison*)
Okay, one at a time.

FUTURE STUDENT ONE

He fought for the rights of African Americans to vote.

FUTURE STUDENT TWO

He was the first field secretary for the NAACP in Mississippi.

FUTURE STUDENT THREE

He was shot and the White man that killed him walked free.
(*All STUDENTS gasp as if ashamed or shocked. The bell rings in the middle of the commotion.*)

TEACHER

So, we'll pick this up tomorrow? Okay, don't forget that tomorrow we have a lesson with our sister school in Spain, so brush up on your Spanish verb conjugation.
(*Students all nod their heads and rush out of class*)

FUTURE STUDENT ONE

(*Walking down the hall with a few other students*)
Today is January 31, 2055, and it's the day we open it. We've waited many generations to have this opportunity, and I'm so glad that I have the chance to experience something that was so important to those who came before me. See, my grandmother was on the steering committee of the Kiamsha Youth Empowerment Organization back in 2005 when they decided to bury this piece of history for future generations.
(*Shows peers a dirty box*)
They wanted us to be able to look at our history to see if we have made any progress in the struggle for absolute freedom and equality. So, today, the members of Kiamsha's after school program at my school are opening the time capsule left for us. It's been 50 years.
(*Students smile and give each other hi-fives. They gather around the box, open it in amazement, and begin to pull out things from today, including a video tape, DVD, audio tape, a CD and CD player, pictures of the organization, a Kiamsha notebook, books, etc., and make comments like, "This is old. Can we even play this in the new system?" "Dag, look at what they have on." "Our notebooks are fly compared to theirs." Etc. Look, they left a CD/DVD player. A Student takes the Pathways CD out and plays the opening to Rainbow of Love*)

(*Play opening to Rainbow of Love:
Just as a rainbow comes to make a beautiful symbol of God's promise to us, we have united as a rainbow to represent the fruit of the spirit. Love, Joy, Peace, Patience, longsuffering, goodness, faithfulness, gentleness, meekness and self-control. The youth of Kiamsha are here to show the world that every Black male is not in jail or on their way to jail, every Latino is not in a gang, and every young girl is not*

pregnant. Young People, there is another way, the right way. Once positive objectives have been enforced and successfully accomplished, then and only then will we be stamped with a glorious seal of well-done. This seal will stand for non-violence in our schools and communities, no more babies having babies, no more corruption of our young minds by our elders, no more crack houses and disrespect for our mothers and sisters. Our seal will stand for no more of our Black men being portrayed as thugs and delinquents. No more ignorance about the history of America. This seal means that our ancestors will be glorified with all honor. Our homes will be filled with loving and nurturing families, males will again be referred to as men. Our women of today will be looked upon as gifts from God that regenerate our generation. Our neighborhoods will have many organizations like Kiamsha that promote self-discipline, self-control, and the blending of generations to empower our youth. And oh my goodness, when this day comes, there will be love in America. A beautiful symphony of brotherhood and sisterhood that is transformed into a Rainbow of Love.)

(Students look shocked as they listen as if they cannot imagine a time when the world was ever like what they just heard. They only know the world like it is for them today.)

FUTURE STUDENT TWO

I see why they fought so hard for the future generations and why Kiamsha is all over the world now. We have to do the same thing to live up to what they hoped for.

FUTURE STUDENT ONE

My grandmother always said that the world we live in today is a result of all the dedication and conviction of her generation. I guess I just couldn't believe it until now.

TEACHER

You know what I think you all should do? You should write a letter to all the Kiamsha members from years ago and to all the elders still living from that generation to let them know how things have changed.

FUTURE STUDENT TWO

Yes, we can just type it and send it over the internet, and all the television and radio stations will automatically receive it!

FUTURE STUDENT THREE

Don't you think they can see how things are different from fifty years ago?

TEACHER

Sure, but they dedicated so much time and energy to making the world a better place for you, and I'm sure they want to hear what you think about their contributions.

FUTURE STUDENT THREE

Oh, okay. Cool.
         (They sit down to write.)

ALL STUDENTS
(Next shot, they are all beside each other in a row and begin to read the letter)
To all those who cared about us before you even knew our names:
(Play the instrumental of Rainbow of Love. Students read while music plays.)
Just as you showed others how a rainbow comes to make a beautiful symbol of God's promise to us, we have united as a rainbow to represent the fruit of the spirit you embodied. The youth of Kiamsha today are showing the world that all the negative stereotypes once placed on our people have diminished. Every Black male is not in jail or on his way to jail, every Latino is not in a gang, and every young girl is not pregnant. Our young people have found another way, the right way. Through your teaching and your dedication to preserving future generations, people around the world have begun to see that once positive objectives have been enforced and successfully accomplished, then and only then will we be stamped with a glorious seal of well-done. This seal now stands for non-violence in our schools and communities, a significant decrease in the use of drugs and alcohol, and a "drastic" drop in the amount of young, unmarried ladies having children. Young minds are no longer corrupted by our elders, instead, elders are seen as trees of wisdom that branch out to encourage and strengthen us. The only place we can see a crack house is in a history book. Our textbooks and curricula are inclusive of the history of *all* Americans. Instead of our Black men being portrayed as thugs and delinquents, they are now seen as pillars of society who are respected and honored. No one is ignorant about the history of America. Your seal also meant that our ancestors would be glorified with all honor, and we would have it no other way.
(Display pictures of ancestors in background)
Our homes are now filled with loving and nurturing families, and males are referred to as men. Our women of today are looked upon as gifts from God that regenerate our generations.
(Shot in background of boys rushing to open the door of a classroom for a young lady)
Internationally, our neighborhoods now have many organizations like Kiamsha that promote self-discipline, self-control, and the blending of generations to empower youth. On today, there is now love in America, a love that is still growing and maturing every day but a love that your generation hoped for. We, the youth of Kiamsha and many other youth organizations around the world, have united in a beautiful symphony of brotherhood and sisterhood that is transformed into your rainbow of love.
(Performance ends with teacher and students hugging and interacting, then leaving the room while music slowly fades out)

END PLAY

Script Credits

Enslavement to Slavery to Freedom—As the Youth See It
An Educational Film and Resource for Schools and Communities

Conceptualized and compiled by Barbara Spencer Dunn

Thanks to:
The Association for the Study of African American Life and History, Inc. (ASALH) for providing all the research to accomplish this educational teaching tool

Sheila Y. Flemming, President, ASALH 2005

Sylvia Cyrus-Albritton, Executive Director, ASALH

Korey Kowers Brown, Historian, Researcher, and Member of ASALH
Co-Editor, 2005 ASALH Black History Theme Products

Daryl Michael Scott, Historian, Researcher, and ASALH Executive Council Member
Co-Editor, 2005 ASALH Black History Theme Products

Michael Childs, Historian and Life Member of ASALH
Researcher, ACT FIVE Decade Research in Script

Kim Pearson, ASALH Life Member
Editor, 2005 ASALH Black History CD ROM

Yohuru Williams, ASALH Life Member and Barbara Spencer Dunn
Co-Author, Film Curriculum Activity Guide

Ida E. Jones, ASALH Life Member
Co-Editor, Black History Bulletin

Vincent DeForest, National Park Service

Largo Senior High School, Prince George's County, Maryland

Kiamsha Youth Empowerment Organization, Prince George's County, Maryland

Film Cast:
Student One: Tiffany Clarke
Student Two: Renada Johnson
Student Three: Don Matthews
Student Four: Shanae Williams

Speeches, Quotes, and Statements Read by:

Opening Statement	Barbara Spencer Dunn
Voice of Reason, Dr. Carter G. Woodson	Carlvern Dunn
Voice of Reason Today	Carlvern Dunn
W.E.B. DuBois	Sulaiman Harris
Booker T. Washington	Benjamin Lucas
William Monroe Trotter	D' Andre Devon Bynum, Kenneth Akil Dickins
Marcus Garvey	Dwight Jones
Ida B. Wells Barnett	Markita Jeter
Martin Luther King	Kenneth Akil Dickins
Medgar Evers	Benjamin Lucas
Angela Davis	Andrea Latney

Production Staff:
Barbara Spencer Dunn, Executive Producer
Lori Leah Croom, Production Director
Kenneth Little, Jr., Director of Photography/Producer
D' Andre Bynum, Co-Producer
Opiyo Okeyo, Editor
Vincent DeForest, Curator and Historic Perspective Director

Musical Scores:
All songs written, arranged, and co-produced by Mico Spencer Scott
Songs co-produced by Don Williams: "Love Ye One Another," "Pathways to Freedom" and "Rainbow of Love"

Harriet Tubman Monologue in Act One excerpted from:
Kiamsha: The Play ©2000 written by Ersky Freeman

Future from Kiamsha's Perspective Written by:
Tiffany Spriggs, Kacey Williams

Extended Future Conclusion from Kiamsha's Perspective Written by:
Luther Davis, Melvette Melvin Davis, Don Matthews, Shanae Williams

Songs Performed by:
"Network to Freedom Performers" (formerly "Network to Freedom Youth Singers")

Notes

[1] Oakes, J., Rogers, J., Silver, D., & Goode, J. (2004). *Separate and Unequal 50 Years After Brown: California's Racial "Opportunity Gap."* Los Angeles, CA: UCLA/IDEA, Institute for Democracy, Education, and Access.

[2] Oakes, J., Rogers, J., Silver, D., Valladares, S., Terriquez, V., McDonough, P, et al. (2006). *Removing the Roadblocks: Fair College Opportunities for All California Students.* Los Angeles, CA: UC/ACCORD & UCLA/IDEA.

[3] Oakes, J., Rogers, J., Silver, D., Valladares, S., Terriquez, V., McDonough, P, et al. (2006). *Removing the Roadblocks: Fair College Opportunities for All California Students.* Los Angeles, CA: UC/ACCORD & UCLA/IDEA.

[4] Oakes, J., Rogers, J., Silver, D., Valladares, S., Terriquez, V., McDonough, P, et al. (2006). *Removing the Roadblocks: Fair College Opportunities for All California Students.* Los Angeles, CA: UC/ACCORD & UCLA/IDEA.

[5] Spencer, J. (2006). *Balancing the Equation: African American Students' Opportunity to Learning Mathematics with Understanding in Two Central City Schools.* (Unpublished Doctoral Dissertation.) University of California, Los Angeles.

ABOUT THE AUTHOR

BARBARA SPENCER DUNN is the executive director of the Kiamsha Youth Empowerment Organization in Prince George's County, Maryland. She coordinates conferences, workshops, and training sessions that empower youth and parents through education about history, social action, and personal responsibility. Mrs. Dunn is also a consultant for the Association for the Study of African American Life and History (ASALH), founded in 1915 by Dr. Carter G. Woodson, the Father of Black History.

******

Mrs. Barbara Spencer Dunn is a descendant of Scott and Tabby Devereux, enslaved on the Monte Verdi Plantation in Rusk County, Texas. Scott and Tabby's daughter Mary is the mother of Phoebe Devereux. Phoebe married Green Lewis, who was also enslaved on the Monte Verdi Plantation, and they gave birth to Jennie Lewis, who married Sim Spencer. Sim and Jennie gave birth to Vernon Spencer, who married Novella Ball. Novella and Vernon are the parents of Barbara Spencer Dunn, the wife of Carl M. Dunn (mother of Carlvern (Paula) and Byron Dunn and Rhonda Evans).

The Monte Verdi Plantation is a tourist site, and the Devereux collection is without doubt one of the most complete records of any antebellum Texas slave plantation. It is rich with primary source material on early Georgia, Alabama, and Texas. Some items date from the eighteenth century. The items are most numerous for the period from 1840 to 1856 when Julien Sidney Devereux (1805-1856), slave owner at the time (son of former slave owner John William Devereux (1769-1847)), lived in Texas in Montgomery and Rusk Counties. Mrs. Dunn and several of her relatives visited the plantation for the first time in June 2010, and their family photo taken on the plantation is the official descendants photo on the Monte Verdi Plantation website: www.monteverdiplantation.com.

This curriculum and educational DVD are resources designed to help teachers, advisors, mentors, and parents lead students through activities that take a critical look at the history of people of African descent in an effort to help students incorporate these facts into their knowledge of United States history. By exploring these missing pieces of United States history that have largely been ignored in the textbooks, we hope that all who engage in this educational project will come to a better understanding of their individual "points of reference" and help move the discussion of slavery to a productive place in the United States and around the world.

The release of this first edition of *Before and Beyond the Niagara Movement:—As the Youth See It* (2011) is aligned with four significant historical events: (1) the year 2011 has been proclaimed by the United Nations General Assembly as the International Year for People of African Descent; (2) it is the 150th anniversary of the Civil War, the war that ended slavery in the United States of America; (3) it is the 25th anniversary of the Martin Luther King, Jr. Day of Service; and (4) it is the 10th anniversary of National Mentoring Month, celebrated in the month of January.

It is my hope that after venturing out to use this document as a guide to teach, or even to pursue personal study, you will recall many of the untruths you may have been taught or passed on to others and take personal responsibility to re-parent and re-educate yourself so we can come together with a clarion call to help make this world a better place to live for all people. This is a call to re-educate "we the people," and this document is a resource dedicated to the youth of Kiamsha as a means for them to continue to perpetuate the legacy of Dr. Carter Godwin Woodson, who is not only the Father of Black History but also a pioneer of multiculturalism. *Enjoy your journey.*

Made in the USA
Charleston, SC
05 September 2014